Congress and the Rent-Seeking Society

Congress and the Rent-Seeking Society

Glenn R. Parker

Ann Arbor

THE UNIVERSITY OF MICHIGAN PRESS

1999   1998   1997   1996   4   3   2   1

A CIP catalog record for this book is available from the British Library.

Library of Congress Cataloging-in-Publication Data

Parker, Glenn R., 1946–
    Congress and the rent-seeking society / Glenn R. Parker.
      p.   cm.
    Includes bibliographical references and index.
    ISBN 0-472-10662-7 (hardcover : alk. paper)
    1. United States. Congress. 2. Legislators—United States.
3. Pressure groups—United States. 4. Campaign funds—United
States. 5. Political corruption—United States. 6. Rent (Economic
theory) 7. Transfer payments—United States. 8. Social choice—
United States.   I. Title.
JK1021.P37   1996
324'.4'0973—dc20   95-42912
                                               CIP

To my family: Suzie, Chris, and Rocky

Acknowledgments

I am indebted to several scholars and friends who offered helpful advice and encouragement in the early stages of this study: Bruce Benson, Morris Fiorina, John Lott, and Barry Weingast. I am especially indebted to Richard Fenno and Gordon Tullock who read the initial version of this manuscript and offered critical insights and suggestions. I hope that the completed book does justice to their wisdom. The manuscript has also benefited from the comments of Michael Munger and Jack Knight; their remarks helped to sharpen the focus of the manuscript and clarify the importance of the ideas contained within it. Bob Tollison kept me abreast of the latest developments in the rent-seeking literature so that I could take advantage of the growth in research in this area of public choice. I also want to express my appreciation to the Fulbright Scholar Program for my appointment as the John Adams Professor of American Studies at the University of Nijmegen in the Netherlands during 1994. The award enabled me to refine and polish many of the ideas contained in this book, and my colleagues at the University of Nijmegen served as a valuable audience, if not a captive one. Finally I want to thank Colin Day for shepherding this book through its inception to its publication; no one could have done it better.

Contents

Introduction

While the evolution of political institutions can assume many different forms—for example, shifts in the locus of power (decentralization)—such transformations inevitably entail changes in institutional rules and arrangements. James Buchanan and Gordon Tullock (1962) alerted us to the possibility that institutional arrangements reflect the needs of those within the institution as well as serving the broader societal interests for which the institution was created. Thus, the evolution of institutional arrangements is likely to reflect personal as well as societal interests. In addition, as institutions evolve unanticipated (latent) consequences always seem to arise. Institutional rules designed to further one or several purposes often produce still other results, some of which may be antithetical to the original intent of the institutional rules themselves! For example, increases in the congressional travel allowance, designed to allow legislators to spend more time in their constituencies, also has resulted in an enhanced role for committee and personal staffs in policy making.

These two observations about institutional evolution—the role of personal as well as collective interests in shaping institutional arrangements and the appearance of latent consequences or secondary effects in the evolution of political institutions—raise a number of questions of particular interest to political scientists. Have our political institutions become too accommodative to the personal interests of political elites? To what extent has institutional service changed over time? How have institutional arrangements shaped the behavior of those in need of governmental services and the behavior of those supplying such services? This book attempts to explore these questions but not from the perspective of conventional political science. Rather, my approach will employ theories and concepts drawn from the field of public choice.

The reader should be forewarned that public choice theories, built upon the basic economic assumption of self-interest, tend to assume a rather healthy skepticism toward the motives of politicians and the actions of government. While this brand of skepticism may be construed as blatant cynicism by some, public choice theories (or theorists, for that matter) rarely pass judgments on politicians—they are perfectly willing to leave it up to the empirical world to prove them wrong. One expression of this skepticism is the proposition advanced by some public choice theorists that society has evolved into a collection of privilege-seeking (special) interests, each attempting to gain economic advantage through governmental action. Surprisingly, perhaps, the implications for political institutions operating within such an environment have yet to be addressed. This is the focus of this inquiry: the evolution of political institutions, specifically Congress, within a rent-seeking society.

For years it has been the contention of economists that groups seek to obtain wealth transfers under the aegis of the state. This premise has given rise to the term *rent seeking* to describe the activities involved in obtaining economic advantage through the political process. Special interests are viewed as seeking policies that earn them supracompetitive profits in the marketplace—a level of profit that could not be obtained without government help. Such behavior on the part of special interests often exercises a corrupting influence on all who participate in the political process. For example, in obtaining government-granted economic privileges, special interests may engage in the outright bribery of public officials, or their efforts may entail something equally pernicious, what Dennis Thompson (1993, 369) has referred to as "mediated corruption" because the acts are mediated through the political process. Mediated corruption is characterized by politicians (1) receiving "political gain" (goods primarily usable in the political process); (2) improperly providing benefits by acting as an intermediary attempting to influence other officials to serve (a constituent's) private interests; and (3) engaging in exchanges that damage the democratic process, typically by bypassing that process altogether (Thompson 1993). No one can be very sanguine about this state of affairs since it contains the seeds of abuse (e.g., the trading of money for legislation) and favoritism. The virtues we often associate with the interplay of groups in politics (see, for example, Truman 1951) may also pose threats to democratic rule (see, for example, Lowi 1969). The large sums of money involved in campaigns, the economic benefits of regulations and government programs, and the discretion enjoyed by legislators (Parker 1992a) provide ripe conditions for biasing policy outcomes to benefit economic interests at the expense of the larger society.

There are a number of implications for political institutions operating in a rent-seeking society; for example, rent seeking reduces citizens' respect for political institutions, damages the esteem of all who serve in these institutions, creates conditions that encourage unethical behavior, and increases the costs of government. Generally speaking, rent-seeking behavior creates external costs that are borne by others than those engaged in extracting rents for, or from, special interests. *Externalities* is the term used to refer to external costs and external benefits, pecuniary as well as nonpecuniary. Externalities can arise in economic situations where an individual's pursuit of his or her own self-interest results in costs or benefits to others. Since these costs and benefits are external to the individual (or individuals) who caused them, they are termed *externalities.* Of course, no harmful or beneficial effect is really external to the world since some person or persons always suffer or enjoy these effects. What converts a harmful or beneficial effect into an externality is that the cost of bringing the effect to bear on the decisions of one or more of the interacting persons is too high to make it worthwhile to do so. Simply put, it costs more to correct the problem than it is worth.

The composition of institutions and the nature of institutional arrangements can evolve in ways that are dysfunctional to the long-term interests of society, and even the functioning of these institutions, thereby creating external costs to society. A central question explored in this inquiry is whether over-time membership changes in Congress (specifically, the House of Representatives) have altered its composition by increasing the proportion of members who spend excessive amounts of money to obtain legislative office, exploit the system and its institutional arrangements for financial gain, and invest heavily in rent-seeking activities. These are the troubling symptoms associated with the adverse selection of politicians for service in Congress.[1]

My discussion of the impact of the rent-seeking society begins with the premise that the intrinsic returns associated with legislative service are significant factors in motivating legislators to seek congressional careers and, once in Congress, in sustaining those same careers. *Intrinsic returns encompass the on-the-job consumption of the nonmaterial rewards associated with public service;* they include (but are not limited to) such things as the prestige and respect that accompanies elective office, the power and influence wielded by officeholders, and the visibility and prominence accorded political elites. These returns are critical to sustaining the daily activities of politicians, many of which entail large personal sacrifices and high opportunity costs.

---

1. Clearly, the emergence of trends symptomatic of adverse selection does not assure that, once in office, legislators will engage in the types of behavior that are detrimental to the effective functioning of a political institution. Despite the emergence of conditions characteristic of adverse selection, a number of mechanisms are capable of moderating such behavior—for example, the intrinsic returns from legislative service and the establishment of sunk investments in political reputations. These mechanisms, as well as others, are explored at length in chapter 7.

As long as government service is highly valued, politicians interested in officeholding per se—the intrinsic rewards or returns from governmental service—can be expected to vigorously seek positions in political institutions and then to hold on to them tenaciously. This normally reduces the pool of candidates for political office to prominent politicians with sterling reputations and records of governmental service. In other words, when government service is highly valued for the intrinsic benefits accompanying officeholding, competition from esteemed politicians normally crowds out those who relish officeholding for reasons other than the career it offers. On the other hand, if institutional service is not highly valued, perhaps due to the low public esteem of the institution, then the intrinsic returns from governmental service will be insufficient to attract esteemed politicians.

The notion that there are intrinsic rewards to public service implies that legislators are motivated by more than material or financial gain. This serves to expand conventional economic assumptions: many economic treatments of politics tend to view politicians as seeking financial gain. For example, Susan Rose-Ackerman contends that "politicians tradeoff gains in personal income against reelection probabilities and may use special interest money for personal enrichment or for campaign spending" (1978, 10; see, also, McCormick and Tollison 1981). From this perspective, individuals seek political office for the material rewards that accompany public service: recruits merely weigh the costs of service against the financial gains. Even electoral competition can be given an economic interpretation: it serves to restrain politicians from "taking too much." "The role of competition," George Stigler has contended, "is not to please voters or customers—it always pays to do that—but to eliminate unnecessary returns to the party or enterprise functionaries" (1972, 96).

While the financial rewards to legislative service cannot be ignored, there is little systematic evidence that such rewards dominate the actions of more than a small segment of Congress. However, *preferences* for monetary gain may be growing within the institution. Moreover, if the intrinsic returns from officeholding were to decline, then the financial rewards of legislative service might become far more important in influencing legislative behavior. As a result, potential recruits preferring the intrinsic returns from congressional service to the financial returns might look elsewhere to establish or further their political careers, and longtime consumers of the intrinsic returns of public service might leave office for more rewarding opportunities. These problems—the entrance and exit of politicians with contrasting appetites for the material and intrinsic rewards of public service—are fundamental issues in the evolution of political institutions and are subjected to empirical study in this inquiry.

While my approach to the issue of legislative recruitment is unique to conventional political science, questions about office-seeking behavior have occupied the attention of congressional scholars for decades. There are a number of ways in which the study of recruitment to legislative office has been approached, but three of the most widely used involve personality theory, the structure of office opportunities, and the existence of political goals (e.g., public policy). From the perspective of personality research, certain psychological dispositions incline individuals to seek political office. One of the most notable advocates of this approach is James D. Barber (1965) who applied this approach to the study of recruitment to the Connecticut state legislature. Relying upon personal interviews; self-administered questionnaires; and a variety of demographic, electoral, and background data, Barber identified four types of legislators: (1) those motivated by the drama of politics ("spectators"), (2) the development of financially rewarding contacts ("advertisers"), (3) civic duty ("reluctants"), and (4) the production of legislation ("lawmakers"). Barber suggested that motivations linked to psychological (personal) needs and predispositions toward politics in general incline individuals to seek political office and to adopt one (or a mixture of) these four legislative styles.

Another perspective on recruitment to legislative office is supplied by Joseph Schlesinger (1966). Central to Schlesinger's study is the observation that political opportunities are structured by a hierarchy of political offices that characterizes the routes politicians follow as they advance in their careers:

> Each politician must work within an opportunity structure that he cannot alter . . . . A politician continually makes decisions which affect his own ability to advance. He must choose his party, time his entry into politics, select his constituency, decide which offices to run for. The sum of these decisions by politicians everywhere certainly affects the general character of the system, but the individual politician, like the producer under conditions of perfect competition who cannot affect the prices of his products, is unable to affect the general structure of opportunities (1966, 19).

Finally, recruitment can involve the interplay of more personal goals. For example, Richard Fenno (1973) has suggested that the desire to formulate "good public policy" or to become a powerful legislator motivates legislators to select career opportunities (e.g., committee assignments) that enhance the realization of such goals.

These perspectives on recruitment and their variants (see, for example, Canon 1990) shed considerable light on why individuals pursue legislative office, but they seem to give little attention to the intrinsic returns from legislative service. As a result, perhaps, the intrinsic returns of legislative service have gone largely unappreciated by most congressional scholars and observers. One of the objectives of this study is to elevate interest in and concern over these returns and to show how they have been affected by the rent-seeking society.

This inquiry also explores another important question addressed historically by political scientists: what is the impact of popular respect and esteem (or the lack thereof) on the functioning of political institutions? For decades scholars have debated the effects of declining (or low levels of) institutional esteem, but little empirical research has resulted. "That the public's view of political life affects who chooses a political career has been a topic of much speculation," Kenneth Prewitt observed more than two decades ago, "though, unfortunately, infrequent systematic investigation" (1970, 98). This study proposes a linkage between institutional esteem and the motivations and behavior of individual legislators: public regard for Congress affects the intrinsic returns from legislative service; these returns, in turn, guide the decisions of politicians whether to invest and how much (time, resources) to invest in a congressional career. In short, the intrinsic returns to congressional service may influence decisions to seek or leave office on the part of dedicated public servants. These returns are, at least partially, a function of the public esteem accorded the institution.

In chapter 1, I attempt to integrate the literature developed by political scientists with respect to the behavior of interest groups in politics with the literature developed recently by public choice economists on rent seeking (see, for example, Buchanan, Tollison, and Tullock 1980). The assumptions and hypotheses underlying the study are discussed in chapter 2, and the role of rent seeking in congressional scandals is examined in chapter 3. Chapter 4 is devoted to defining the question of adverse selection and exploring how the evolution of Congress might be afflicted by the rent-seeking activities of groups and individuals. Chapter 5 explores the in-office behavior of legislators to determine the extent to which different generations of legislators engage in the types of activities that are generally discussed by economists under the rubric of "rent seeking" (raising and spending campaign funds) and how that behavior changes during the course of a congressional career.[2] Chapter 6 examines

---

2. Campaign spending and receipts are not normally construed as rent seeking by political scientists since *all* prospective recruits must endure very costly elections; hence, the money used in campaigns is necessary to obtain office. From the perspective of the

patterns in congressional exits over time. A major question in this chapter is how declining institutional esteem, and increases in rent seeking, affect the departure of career politicians. Chapter 6 also explores the rent-seeking behavior of legislators facing their last term of office—a prime time for opportunistic behavior. Chapter 7 discusses several mechanisms that might effectively deter legislators from taking advantage of their positions in the legislature.

Some might question the application of economic theory to an issue normally described and discussed through contemporary political science terms. After all, I am arguing that declines in public regard for Congress and increases in interest group activity in the legislative arena make the job of the "legislator" less attractive thereby precipitating the retirement of some of our most experienced legislators and deterring dedicated and respected public servants from seeking congressional service. The value of economics is that it simplifies the complex dynamics underlying these interrelationships among institutional esteem, interest group activity, office attraction, recruitment, and retirement decisions and integrates these variables into a more parsimonious explanation. The economic model examined in this study envisions intrinsic returns as responding to fluctuations in the esteem accorded legislative office and levels of rent seeking. Declines in the esteem accorded legislative office and increased rent seeking eventually reduce the intrinsic returns to legislative service to the point that only those who can obtain positive returns (under these conditions) remain in office. The returns to congressional service are increasingly likely to be more material than intrinsic when rent-seeking activity is high and institutional esteem is low. Thus, those who obtain positive returns in a legislature low in institutional esteem but high in rent-seeking activity are likely to be attracted to legislative service more by material rewards than intrinsic ones.

In addition, the application of economics to issues of institutional evolution yields insights into the rational behavior of politicians and interest groups that might escape the notice of those working solely within the confines of either economics or political science. "One result of the economist's approach is an increased capacity for suggesting

---

rent-seeking literature, campaign spending reflects a major consequence of rent seeking: since the extralegal (or quasilegal) pay is so attractive (i.e., rents), individuals overspend to obtain office. For instance, many legislators spend three or four times the explicit salary attached to the office in running for reelection. As for campaign receipts, they may encompass payoffs for past or future treatment in the legislature, committees, or the bureaucracy. This is not to say that campaign expenditures and receipts serve these and only these purposes; my point is that we have no assurance that these activities do not serve such rent-seeking aims.

startling possibilities, counterintuitive results, and a greater ability to investigate boundary conditions and perverse outcomes" (Mitchell and Munger 1991, 314). For example, the lack of widespread legislative effort to restore public confidence in, and respect for, Congress reflects the "free rider" problem endemic to the provision of collective goods (see, for example, Olson 1965) as well as the political problems involved in most reform efforts (see, for instance, Davidson and Oleszek 1977). Finally, the application of economics enables us to make use of basic theories in microeconomics and gain the benefit of their generalizability, predictability, and simplicity—supplying a useful analytic framework to discuss, describe, and explore the rational behavior of legislators. In short, a major benefit of applying an economic perspective is that it sheds light on questions and yields insights into still other hypotheses that have heretofore received little or no notice.

Unfortunately, economists have normally treated Congress as an unimportant factor in the translation of group demands into public policy; the legislature is seen as simply a mechanism for auctioning off policies to the highest bidders. For example, George Stigler has written that "whatever the governmental form, equilibrium in the political marketplace for legislative goods and harms is determined by the nature and composition of the politically effective coalitions and the size and nature of the programs they achieve" (1988, x–xi). From the perspective of political scientists, however, institutions, like the legislature, matter. Thus, this book approaches an area of study—legislatures—important to political scientists with the analytic tools of the economist to explore the evolution of Congress within a society dominated by rent-seeking interests. The approach may be economic, but the substance of this inquiry is clearly within the purview of political science. The problem underlying this inquiry—namely, the evolution of political institutions— seems to warrant such a hybrid approach. The task involves more than just relating variables used in political science to those used in economics; it also entails the reformulation of research questions in terms of economic theory and the integration of economic and political concepts. It is this process that generates insights into politics and the rational behavior of legislators.

In conclusion, the major objective of this inquiry is to explore the long-term effects of the rent-seeking society on the evolution of the U.S. Congress, and in the process, to identify potential or emerging problems. In an earlier book (Parker 1992a), I argued that institutional changes in Congress were designed to maximize legislator discretion. In that study I demonstrated that there were at least two positive consequences of a discretion-maximizing legislature: the enhanced attractiveness of a congressional career and the increased productivity of Congress. I noted, however, that such latitude also yields opportunities for legislators to exploit their discretion to enhance their wealth by engaging in illegal, quasiethical, or socially undesirable practices. The present book, then, is an attempt to explore the "dark side" of a discretion-maximizing legislature: how does a persisting demand for preferential treatment by organized interests affect the evolution of an institution where its members have considerable freedom and influence in the making of public policy?

While corruption can be intertwined with rent seeking, this is not a book about corruption in total, or even in part; rather, it is a study designed to better inform students of politics of problems in the evolution of political institutions in general and of Congress in particular. The underlying research question is whether the growth and maturation of the rent-seeking society has created institutional problems in the evolution of the membership of the U.S. Congress.[3]

---

3. Economists are relatively silent as to the timing of the emergence of the rent-seeking society in the United States, though Professors Shughart and Tollison (1981) have reported evidence that the liberalization of corporate chartering laws between 1837 and 1913 seems to have been a response to rent seeking by state manufacturing interests. I prefer to think of the rent-seeking society as having always been with us but as increasing its hold on politics in recent decades. For example, there is evidence in the early years of the nation that the political process was used to obtain favorable economic treatment (e.g., tariffs). As political institutions respond to the growth in rent-seeking activity (e.g., campaign contributions) they exhibit an evolution in rules, organization, and membership. It is this last issue, the evolution of the membership of Congress, that occupies the attention of this inquiry.

CHAPTER 1

Legislators, Interest Groups, and Rent Seeking

The purpose of this chapter is to integrate the literature on rent seeking—primarily drawn from the public choice literature—with the traditional study of interest groups and legislators by political scientists. It serves to acquaint the reader with the economic terms and concepts used in the study of group behavior and rent seeking as well as current thinking about the relationship between group action and policy outcomes. The study of interest groups has long historical roots within political science. James Madison, for example, recognized groups as a central focus of political action. His view, as expressed in several of *The Federalist Papers,* was that groups were united by some common interest adverse to the rights of citizens or to the aggregate interests of the broader community. Clearly, Madison was, like many of today's economists, concerned about the "mischiefs" promulgated by groups on the rights of others and the collective interests of society. While he believed that groups were the inevitable result of human nature and that their activities and development could not be checked naturally, Madison proposed that competition among groups, or "factions" as he called them, would serve as an effective constraint. Simply put, competition among selfish interests for political power would limit the gains that any interest could hope to realize. This idea—that group influence is constrained by the actions and competition of others, either voters or other interests—is central to several contemporary economic theories of group action (Becker 1983; Denzau and Munger 1986; Peltzman 1976). This is not to suggest that Madison's thinking can be construed as either elementary public choice or political economy. My point is rather that some of the ideas underlying Madison's notion of group behavior can be easily accommodated within an economic framework.

The view that governmental policy and governments themselves were inextricably linked to the behavior of interest groups was advanced further by Arthur Bentley (1908), who envisioned society as little more than an assemblage of the groups that comprised it. Bentley's view was the driving force behind one of the first extensive, empirical analyses of the role of groups in politics and society, David B.

Truman's *The Governmental Process* (1951). Truman characterized government in many of the same terms used by Bentley. Government, according to Truman, was an aggregation of groups, interacting with one another as well as groups outside of government. "[Groups] . . . are so intimately related to the daily functioning of those constitutionalized groups—legislatures, chief executives, administrative agencies, and even courts—that make up the institution of government that the latter cannot be adequately described if these relationships are not recognized as the weft of the fabric" (1951, 46).

Truman's work represents a break with past views of special interests since he tended to portray groups in a rather benign, favorable light—in sharp contrast to Madison's skepticism. While Truman cannot be accused of fostering a sublime view of groups, many theories and research on groups that followed his work have tended to view groups as far less threatening, and perhaps even beneficial, to society. For example, Lester Milbrath's classic study, *The Washington Lobbyists,* suggested that group influence over politicians was greatly exaggerated: "Lobbyists and lobbying groups have a very limited ability to control the selection of officials or to affect the likelihood that an official can keep or enhance his position" (1963, 342). According to Milbrath, the influence of groups in politics was merely a function of the fact that "members of groups are citizens and the political system is designed to respond to the influence of their votes" (342). Milbrath claimed that the negative image of interest groups and lobbyists resulted from the efforts of the press to play up "the unsavory and sensational aspects of lobbying, printing few stories about the ordinary, honest lobbyist and his workaday activities—presumably because they would not 'sell' " (298). Not all of the studies of interest groups present such a benign view, however.

A far more caustic view of groups, and one shared by many contemporary public choice economists, was offered by E. E. Schattschneider (1975) who attacked groups for distorting the "public's interest" and promoting policies grounded in an upper-class bias. Schattschneider complained that the interest group system was narrow in scope and had few participants and a definite pro-business bias: the ability of business to organize for political action better than other segments of society, and the likelihood that participation in groups would be dominated by those of higher income, education, and status, gave groups an undeniable upper-class bias. Schattschneider's attack on special interests has a vigorous supporter in Theodore Lowi (1969). Lowi grimly contended that government had constantly expanded its role and impact on society while simultaneously and systematically abdicating its power over the direction and substance of public policy to private groups. The result, according to Lowi, has been ineffective policies and a "corruption of modern democratic government" (1969, 287). Lowi cited four ways in which group involvement in politics undermined the linkages between citizens and their government:

1. It deranges and confuses expectations about democratic institutions and reveals a basic disrespect for democracy
2. It renders government impotent, unable to plan
3. It demoralizes government, by replacing concern for justice (doing the "right thing") with concern for jurisdiction (which actors make the decisions)
4. It weakens democratic institutions by opposing formal procedure
   (288–91)

As I have intimated, the study of groups by political scientists has strong parallels with research by economists. Not only do many economists share the same fears as many political scientists—namely, that interest groups and politicians exchange favors that result in policies adverse to the best interests of society—but the methodological tools and data are virtually identical. Differences exist nonetheless. Basically, the contrasts are rooted in the nature of inquiry that separates the two disciplines, namely, differences in explanatory theories and concepts. This distinction surely can be overdrawn since scholars studying group behavior, whether they be economists or political scientists, often include variables drawn from both economics and political science. One important intersection or nexus in the analysis of interest groups by economists and political scientists is the study of rent seeking. In fact, a large proportion of political science research on interest groups can be subsumed within the theoretical framework termed *rent seeking*.

Defining Rent Seeking

Rent seeking is a relatively new concept in economic theory, with much of the research surfacing in the 1970s. The behavior that it explains, however, has always been a part of the political landscape in the United States and elsewhere (see, for example, Krueger 1974), and there is little likelihood that it will disappear or even fade. William Mitchell and Michael Munger provide a useful definition of rent seeking:

> Rent seeking is usually defined as the political activity of individuals and groups who devote scarce resources to the pursuit of monopoly rights granted by governments. The basic propositions of

rent-seeking theory are (1) that the expenditure of resources to gain a transfer is itself a social cost and that (2) the resulting market privileges or rents represent a welfare loss on consumers and taxpayers. The numerous actual actions and policy instruments by which rents are created and conveyed are designed to conceal the gains. They range from outright bribery to sales of subsidies, tax privileges, price supports, tariffs, farm or import quotas, or licenses to the highest bidders, with the proceeds going to officials in the form of higher salaries and perquisites. (1991, 525)

The everyday usage of the word "rent" to describe the monetary collections paid to landlords bears no resemblance to the definition of the term in economics. "Rent is that part of the payment to an owner of resources over and above that which those resources could command in any alternative use" (Buchanan 1980, 4). Simply put, rents are receipts *in excess* of opportunity cost, and there is no necessity to pay the owner of a resource more than the alternative earning power of that resource—that is, more than its opportunity cost. Therefore, rents are unnecessary payments that would not be required to attract resources to a particular employment. For example, if a legislator receives a $2,000 honorarium for presenting a ten-minute speech to a group, the remuneration probably exceeds what the legislator could earn for a comparable amount of effort and time. Such a payment qualifies as a rent.

Rent seeking normally emerges when political or governmental interference with markets creates differentially advantageous positions for those who are able to secure the valuable "rights" to those advantaged positions. An example may make this relationship between rent seeking and the role of government clearer. If an entrepreneur were to organize the production and sale of a new commodity, he or she would be a pure monopolist if no one else were aware of this opportunity for gain. Moreover, the monopoly would continue until others contested the market for this new product. As a monopolist, the entrepreneur would secure a rate of return over and above what he or she might earn in an alternative employment—an "economic rent" on his or her entrepreneurial investment and activity. This signals other non-innovating (but potentially imitating) producers of the commodity to enter the market and sell the new product or some close substitute. The initial monopoly rent obtained by the innovating entrepreneur eventually would be eroded by competition, causing the price of the product to fall. Thus, the dynamics of a competitive market dissipate the rents earned by producers. No dissipation of rents will occur, however, if the entry of other producers into the market is effectively blocked.

If the innovating entrepreneur had also discovered a way to convince the government that he or she "deserved" to be granted an exclusive (monopoly) right by restricting potential entrants, the rent would not have dissipated.[1] "So long as governmental action is restricted largely, if not entirely, to protecting individual rights, personal and property, and enforcing voluntarily negotiated private contracts, the market process dominates economic behavior and ensures that any economic rents that appear will be dissipated by the forces of competitive entry" (Buchanan 1980, 9). Once governmental involvement in the market is apparent, however, attempts will be made to capture these rents, and the resources used in this pursuit will reflect social waste, even if the investments are fully rational for all the participants. (I will have more to say about the social costs of rent seeking in section 3 of this chapter.) Since rents accrue to those who are successful at securing the privilege to engage in some activity, individuals will invest scarce resources to secure either the initial assignment of rights or the replacement of other initial holders through ouster. These "rights" are then codified into governmental licenses, quotas, permits, approvals, franchise assignments, and administrative regulations.

In the rent-seeking world of rational interest groups and politicians, groups demand and political representatives supply wealth transfers. If the informational and organizational costs of these transfers were nonexistent (zero), only transfers that benefited majorities at each stage of the decision-making process would be passed by a legislature in a representative democracy. But the existence of such costs ensures that some groups will be able to organize and acquire information more cheaply than other groups. Therefore, they will be in a better position to influence the supply of wealth transfers. For example, the costs involved in acquiring information relevant to rent seeking involve discovering the effects of a policy on one's personal wealth and identifying others who might join to form a group.[2] "Naturally, the men who stand to gain from exerting

---

1. Monopoly rents should not be confused with the type of postcontractual opportunism that creates appropriable quasi-rents. Monopoly rents represent the increased value of an asset protected from market entry over the value it would have had in an open market, while appropriable quasi-rents can occur without market closure or restrictions placed on rival assets. For example, once installed an asset may be so expensive to remove or so specialized to a particular user that if the price paid to the owner were somehow reduced, the asset's service to that user would not be reduced. The specialization of the installed asset to a particular user, or the high costs of making it available to others, creates a quasi-rent, but no monopoly rent. For an informative analysis of quasi-rents and controlling opportunistic behavior, see Klein, Crawford, and Alchian (1978).

2. Anthony Downs (1957, 253) argues that groups bent upon influencing government need more information than even the most well-informed voters. Hence, they incur

influence in a policy area are the ones who can best afford the expense of becoming expert about it. Their potential returns from influence are high enough to justify a large investment of information" (Downs 1957, 254). This leads politicians to seek policies demanded by well-organized groups at the expense of the more diffuse general public (see Stigler 1971). Clearly, then, the costs of acquiring information and communicating opinions to government officials help to determine the structure of group influence: those who can pay the price are also in a position to "call the tune." Benefiting the few at the expense of the many makes sense in a representative democracy when consideration is given to the costs associated with influencing governmental policy.

Particularly important in this regard are the start-up costs associated with organizing to influence government. Groups that have already incurred start-up costs, or are able to produce legislative pressure as a by-product of performing other functions (Olson 1965), will have a comparative advantage in seeking wealth transfers.[3] For example, groups that have successfully resolved the free-rider problem that plagues collective efforts (e.g., lobbying) stand to gain in obtaining favorable governmental treatment. From this perspective, a small number of producer groups that are able to overcome free riding and other organizational costs should be able to wield considerable influence in determining wealth transfers. As for consumers, they—like most large groups— might suffer from such monopoly-enhancing decisions, but they have no incentive to organize to resist the policies favored by the producers simply because resistance costs more than it is worth.

But what do rent-seeking groups want specifically from government, and what are they willing to exchange for preferential treatment? In the next section, I describe some of the objectives sought by groups in attempting to influence governmental policy in ways advantageous to themselves and the "trades" they make to secure such preferential treatment.

Rent-Seeking Pursuits and Exchanges

The power of government to coerce its citizens provides incentives for rational groups and their leaders to exploit the political process for economic gain. In the rent-seeking paradigm, groups or "industries" as they are sometimes called (see Stigler 1971) pursue four objectives

---

higher data costs: "Each must (1) produce arguments to counter any attacks on him, (2) assault the others' contentions with data of his own, and (3) be informed enough to know what compromises are satisfactory to him."

3. There are a number of ways in which the rent-seeking behavior of groups creates wealth transfers, for example, regulations, tariffs, quotas, and government contracts.

through governmental action: direct subsidies of money, control over the entry of rivals, influence over policies that affect the attractiveness of substitutes and complements to an industry's product, and price-fixing policies beneficial to an industry. Groups do not often enlist the services of government to supply direct cash benefits; instead, they cultivate other ways to employ the coercive powers of the state. The reason is simple: unless the list of beneficiaries can be limited by some acceptable device, the amount of the direct subsidy an industry or group obtains will be quickly dissipated among a growing number of rivals. For example, the inability of the premier universities to exclude other claimants for government-sponsored research funds ensures that they will receive much reduced shares of federal research monies in the long run. Perhaps the most commonly sought government-supplied benefit for groups is control over the entry of rivals. Regulatory policies, for example, can be fashioned to retard the growth of competing industries. In any event, groups seek policies that create monopoly power and therefore generate monopoly-like profits. In pursuit of these objectives, groups seek access to decision makers, election of "friendly" legislators, votes on specific legislation, and bureaucratic favors.

It is not really too surprising that access to decision makers is such a prominent goal for interest groups. After all, power of any degree cannot be obtained by an interest group without access to one or perhaps several key points of decision making within government. The U.S. political system seems unusually accommodating to group demands for access. The federal system establishes more or less independent centers of powers—vantage points that can be exploited in influencing public policy. National parties, and even those in many states, tend to be fragmented coalitions of locally based organizations rather than unified, inclusive structures. Staggered terms of office for political executives and legislators combine with a decentralized legislative process to further multiply the positions (and people) with influence over public policy. Such divided channels of control over public policy ensure a vast array of access points for pressure groups. The demand for access motivates groups to support "sure winners" in legislative elections and to develop mutually beneficial relationships with legislators from districts with group connections (e.g., facilities, plants, members).

One way that groups guarantee themselves a degree of influence over public policy is to populate the legislature (and/or the executive) with officials who are sympathetic toward the groups' objectives and interests. Legislators whose interests and attitudes coincide with those of a group, or whose election is dependent upon group support, can be counted upon to further the interests of that pressure group. In short, both identification and coercion encourage legislators to do a group's bidding.

Legislative votes can easily become the focal point of group pressure. Roll-call decisions provide a test of group strength in the legislature and the reliability and power of its friends within. Legislative decisions are also critical elements in finalizing contractual agreements between legislators and pressure groups; they assure an element of durability to these agreements (Landes and Posner 1975). Since journalists are quick to assail the actions of groups in influencing legislators' decisions and legislators' wrongdoings make headline news in all the media, transactions between legislators and groups are difficult to document and monitor. Vote buying, then, is virtually impossible to uncover though rather spectacular examples of influence peddling remind us that such situations are not at all improbable (see chapter 3). This is, without doubt, one of the least attractive facets of the behavior of pressure groups in American politics, but it may be an external cost of a pluralistic political system.

At times, bureaucratic decisions, rather than legislative ones, are the objects of group influence. Frequently, groups request that their congressional representative intervene in the internal workings of a federal (or state) agency to affect decisions in a way favorable to the group, to reverse decisions adverse to group interests, or simply to speed up the glacial bureaucratic process. Legislators possess the power to deliver these goods as a result of legislative control over what bureaucrats value most—higher budgets and new or broader programs. With respect to Congress, Morris Fiorina has observed that:

> The bureaucracy needs congressional approval in order to survive, let alone expand. Thus, when a congressman calls about some minor bureaucratic decision or regulation, the bureaucracy considers his accommodation a small price to pay for the goodwill its cooperation will produce. (1977, 43)

In sum, legislator intervention may influence bureaucratic decisions thereby enabling rent-seeking groups to obtain economic advantages.

Many times, groups would be content just to hold on to their existing (favored) position within society rather than increase their gains. Hence, groups can often be found trying to protect their privileges rather than extending them. "The primary effect of the friendship and overlapping interests among members (of Congress) and industry is that nothing is done. Most industries do not send their lobbyists to Washington to seek profitable legislation; they send them to Washington to block legislation that might control or cost them more in taxes" (Sherrill 1974 128). Those contesting a group's favored position or advantageous treatment are not always other special interests. Legislatures not only possess the power to create rents, but they can also impose costs that would destroy the private rents that some groups already enjoy. The passage of sharply focused taxes and regulations, for example, can reduce the returns that groups expect to receive.

In order to protect these returns, groups have incentives to strike bargains with legislators to prevent the legislature from exercising its right to impose costs in the form of burdensome restrictions on private groups. Of course these payments to legislators must be lower than the expected losses resulting from compliance with the threatened law or regulation to motivate groups to pursue such exchanges: "If the expected cost of the act threatened exceeds the value of the consideration that private parties must give up to avoid legislative action, they will surrender the tribute demanded of them" (McChesney 1987, 104). Thus, legislators obtain rents by threatening groups with adverse governmental interference. One way in which legislatures can threaten groups is by merely considering legislation deregulating a previously cartelized industry:

> Expected political rents created by earlier regulation are quickly capitalized into firm share prices. If politicians later breach their contract and vote unexpectedly to deregulate, shareholders suffer a wealth loss. Rather than suffer the costs of deregulation, shareholders will pay politicians a sum up to the amount of wealth threatened to have them refrain from deregulating. In fact, one routinely observes payments to politicians to protect previously enacted cartel measures. (McChesney 1987, 105)

Viewed in this light, Congress as well as the bureaucracy impose costs on groups, and politicians gain by mitigating these costs.

In the rent-seeking paradigm, legislation enhancing economic benefits is supplied to interest groups or coalitions that outbid rival seekers for favorable treatment. The price that the victorious group bids is determined both by the value of the legislation to the group (i.e., group members) and the costs of organizing and overcoming the free-rider problem associated with the provision of collective goods. Simply put, legislation is "sold" by the legislature and "bought" by groups benefiting from the legislation. From this perspective, government is the supplier of regulatory services such as price fixing, restriction of entry, subsidies, suppression of substitutes, and promotion of complimentary goods. In exchange for these highly valuable services, regulated industries offer legislators campaign contributions, speaking fees or honoraria, electoral support of industry employees, and perhaps a promise of future employment.

Unlike private sales where there are legal sanctions for nonperformance, there are no legal sanctions for the failure of a legislature to carry out its "bargain" with an interest group. That is, there are no legal mechanisms analogous to a binding long-term contract by which an enacting Congress can prevent a subsequent one from amending legislation in ways unfavorable to a group, or from repealing it altogether! (Such bad faith, by reducing the value of legislation to interest groups [and the benefits it bestows], also imposes costs on members of Congress since the price legislators could demand for enacting such legislation would be lower.) Thus, special interests are not merely satisfied with obtaining legislative agreements—they also want these agreements to be durable. Congressional agreements are quite satisfying in this regard.

There are at least two reasons why congressional-group agreements are durable: procedures for the enactment of legislation increase the cost of repealing it, and an independent judiciary enforces legislation in accordance with the intentions of the enacting legislature. Durability is enhanced by procedural rules, such as the requirement that legislation must be enacted by a majority of the legislators voting. This stipulation makes the passage of legislation both a difficult and time-consuming process because of the transaction costs involved in gaining agreement among a large number of individuals and the variety of veto points in the process. Thus, once a law is passed it is unlikely to be substantially altered or repealed in the immediate future. In addition, durability is promoted by the fact that interest-group legislation is normally fashioned to avoid the requirement of substantial annual appropriations thereby avoiding the necessity for the benefiting groups to "buy" the legislation anew each session.

Since legislation is not self-enforcing, judicial action may be required to assure that legislative intent is being followed. But would a judiciary that is subservient to the *current* members of the legislature uphold the validity of legislation enacted in previous sessions? "Insofar as judges are merely agents of the current legislature," William Landes and Richard Posner observed, "they will utilize their considerable interpretive leeway to rewrite the legislation in conformity with the views of the current rather than the enacting legislature, and they will thereby impair the 'contract' between the enacting legislature and the group that procured the legislation" (1975, 879). In contrast, an *independent* judiciary assures the durability of legislative "deals" because, being independent, it interprets legislation in accordance with the original legislative understanding. To do otherwise would severely damage the courts' independence.

Of course, legislators must gain from such an institutional arrangement for it to persist, and in fact they do benefit. Landes and Posner (1975) argue that the durability of legislation, fostered by legislative procedures and an independent judiciary, serves the function of permitting the capitalization of future returns into the pockets of members of the *current* legislature by increasing the value of, and hence the demand for, legislation. Or, simply put, members in the present legislature are able to increase the "sale" of legislation because the durability of laws increases their value to special interests and therefore the demand. But what do groups supply to entice legislators to produce differentially advantageous benefits?

There are several commodities that groups traffic in: campaign funds, honoraria, jobs, and influence over voters. Reelection is an important force motivating congressional behavior and even the organization of Congress itself (Mayhew 1974). Whatever the private motives legislators might harbor for gaining and remaining in office (money, altruism, power, rents), reelection is basic to the realization of these goals. Even members bent on exercising discretion will need to maintain healthy reelection margins to assure themselves a cushion of electoral support while they pursue their private agendas (see Parker 1992a). Not surprisingly, therefore, campaign contributions often serve as the currency that groups offer legislators: campaign funds help incumbents finance their reelection efforts and mobilize district (or state) voters. Honoraria are far more removed from reelection concerns than campaign funds since they involve direct cash payments that legislators can pocket.[4] Sometimes, groups offer accommodating legislators post employment (see, for example, Eckert 1981). Legislators may join firms as high-level executives or consultants, earning a fine ex ante return on their service to the group while in government. Ethics laws constrain such interchanges between the public and private sectors, but ample opportunities to reward legislators both in and out of office remain.

Groups also use their influence over voters to entice legislators to further group causes. Anthony Downs defines *interest groups* in his model as "leaders who try to get government to adopt some particular policy beneficial to themselves by claiming to represent voters. They seek to implant their views in voters' minds so that they do represent voters; then the government may be impressed enough to aid them" (1957, 88). According to Downs, government needs resources to con-

---

4. For a more detailed discussion of the analysis of honoraria income, see chapter 5. Presently, senators and representatives are prohibited from accepting honoraria as personal income.

vince voters that its policies are beneficial to them and to defend itself from attack by groups who disagree with its policies. To acquire the resources for these tasks, it "sells" favors to those who need governmental action and are willing to pay handsomely for it. In sum, groups supply resources that help legislators remain in office (votes, campaign funds) along with enticements that involve more personal consumption (post employment, honoraria). These goods make the exchanges between rent-seeking groups and legislators possible—and profitable.

The Social Cost of Rent Seeking

A major tenet of the rent-seeking paradigm, and a characteristic that distinguishes "rents" from "profits," is that rent seeking is wasteful from a societal standpoint. The standard model of monopoly helps to illustrate the logic underlying this premise. Figure 1 shows the impact of a monopoly on the price and production of a commodity. When the market price rises above the competitive level ($MC=AC$), those who continue to purchase the product at the new, higher price suffer a loss (L), which is exactly offset by the additional revenue that the sellers obtain at the higher price. Consumers who refuse to buy the product at the higher price also suffer a loss (D), but this loss is not offset by any gain to the sellers. This is what economists refer to as the "deadweight loss" from supracompetitive pricing and is traditionally perceived to be the only social cost of monopolies. The welfare triangle (D) represents a clear

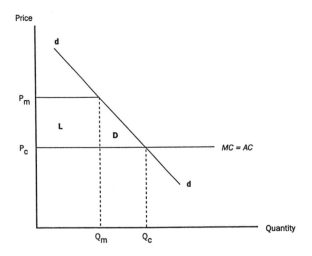

Fig. 1. The social costs of monopoly

loss to society, but the rectangle to its left (L) is merely a transfer from the consumer to the owners of the monopoly. (We may vigorously object to the monopolist's getting rich at our expense, but this does not result in a reduction in the national product.)

The rectangle (L) to the left of the welfare triangle (D) is the income transfer that a successful monopolist can expect to extort from his or her customers. The problem with income transfers is not merely that they *directly* inflict welfare losses on society, but that they lead individuals to employ resources to obtain or prevent such transfers. With so large a prize (the rectangle L), potential monopolists would be willing to invest considerable resources in securing a monopoly. We might anticipate that sellers or producers would invest resources to obtain such a monopoly until the marginal return or the last dollar spent was equal to its likely return: "Entrepreneurs should be willing to invest resources in attempts to form a monopoly until the marginal cost equals the properly discounted return" (Tullock 1980b, 48). In addition, potential customers should be interested in preventing the transfer and therefore should try to influence government officials to that end. Continuous efforts either to break the monopoly or to muscle in on it once the monopoly is established can also be expected. The holders of the monopoly, on the other hand, can be expected to invest considerable resources in defending their control over the transfer.

These expenditures, which may do little more than offset the efforts and expenditures of others, are purely wasteful from the standpoint of society as a whole: they are spent not in increasing wealth but in attempts to transfer (or resist the transfer of) wealth. In addition, the costs incurred by the unsuccessful as well as the successful attempts to obtain the monopoly raise the societal cost of rent seeking. Indeed, "most of the costs are incurred in unsuccessful efforts to obtain a monopoly: the lobbying campaign that fails, the unsuccessful attempt to obtain a bank charter or form a cartel" (Posner 1980, 77). Just as successful theft will stimulate other thieves to greater effort and require greater investment in protective measures (e.g., more police), so each successful establishment of monopoly power stimulates greater diversion of resources to organize (or prevent) further transfers of income.

Some Influences on Rent Seeking

What factors stimulate groups to engage in rent-seeking behavior? Rent seeking is driven by the expected cost and rate of return that such effort is perceived to generate. Several factors help to determine the returns to rent seeking. First, rent seeking is affected by the expected return to *productive effort:* "If rent seeking and productive effort both are re-garded purely as means to obtain goods for consumption, the return to productive effort is the opportunity cost of rent seeking, and anything conducive to a higher value of return serves to diminish the likelihood that the individual will engage systematically in rent seeking" (Orr 1980, 244). That is, if the returns from productive effort are less than those derived from rent seeking, individuals and groups will gravitate to the higher-earning activity—rent seeking. In addition, the size and structure of government, especially the size of the individual chambers (Mc-Cormick and Tollison 1980) and the scope and range of government involvement in the economy, influence the expected returns from rent seeking. Finally, since government activity—taxing, spending, and regu-lating—increases the potential for rents, the perceived supply of acces-sible rents affects estimates of the returns from rent seeking.

We can expect lobbyists to rationally allocate their budgets in purchasing legislative influence so as to maximize the returns from legislation. Whether a particular group can afford the price necessary to capture these returns is a function of its comparative advantage in collecting votes and contributions for legislators and other politicians. The "price" of legislation, in turn, is affected by several factors related to the size of the legislature and its respective chambers. For instance, the costs of influence are less in large as compared to small legislatures because there are a greater number of suppliers of political favors and influence in larger legislatures. Thus, competition among legislators for a share of the market for special interest legislation affects the "broker-age fee" they can demand for supplying rents or wealth transfers. Large legislative chambers, therefore, reduce the monopoly power among suppliers (legislators). In addition, larger legislatures necessar-ily reduce the power of individual legislators; hence, each is likely to have a relatively minor impact on legislative outcomes.

Similarly, bicameralism also affects the returns to interest groups since rent-seeking groups must build support in two legislative chambers, and the costs may be especially high if group supporters are not distrib-uted equally across both houses. When different interests dominate differ-ent chambers, each group holds a veto over legislation. For example, Thomas Gilligan, William Marshall, and Barry Weingast (1989) demon-strate that the Interstate Commerce Act of 1887 was a compromise among many competing groups: shorthaul shippers gained important restrictions on railroad pricing thereby improving their welfare (shorthaul markets are served by a single railroad); river towns and eastern production cen-ters benefited from lessened competition owing to higher longhaul prices (longhaul markets are served by several railroads and are naturally more competitive). This compromise was fostered by the bicameral nature of Congress and the institutional pockets of legislative influence occupied by legislators supportive of the interests of the contending groups. Each special interest dominated a specific committee in the respective congressional chambers: railroads dominated the Senate committee with jurisdiction over the legislation, while shorthaul shippers dominated the corresponding committee in the House. The compromise contained provisions benefiting each special interest so that the package as a whole made each better off than under the status quo: the existence of "committee veto" power assured that any compromise reached among the contending parties would be beneficial to each group.

The expected returns obtained by influencing government are often related to government's role in the affected industry (e.g., government regulation, government purchase of industry output, government antitrust investigations). Although government plays a role in just about all American industries, in some industries the role is so limited that political influence is not worth the cost. In other industries, however, the impact of government might be so extensive that the potential benefits of influence are substantial. But even if government's role is significant, an industry may have difficulty mounting a successful lobbying campaign if there are few incentives for component firms in the industry to contribute resources to the lobbying effort. For instance, in an unconcentrated industry each firm is aware that it will receive the benefits resulting from the policy influence exercised on behalf of the industry whether or not it assumes a share of the costs. Thus, groups weigh the possibility of free riding on the efforts of other special interests when deciding whether or not to devote resources to pressuring government officials. This free-rider hypothesis has been subjected to a clever empirical analysis by Russell Pittman (1977).

Pittman examined the then "secret" contributions to the "Committee to Re-elect the President" (Richard Nixon) between January 1, 1972, and April 6, 1972. These contributions were made with the expectation that the names of the donors would remain secret since only contributions made after April 7, 1972, were to be made public according to law; however, a successful lawsuit by Common Cause forced disclosure of pre-April 7 contributions. The purported secrecy of the contributions encouraged those benefiting from government policy to reveal their indebtedness and their stake in government policy. Pittman regressed the total level of industry contributions on a series of variables representing government regulation of an industry, purchase of industry output, and antitrust investigations of an industry. He found that these characteristics were important factors increasing "secret" contributions among the concentrated industries, but none of these variables influenced contributions among the unconcentrated industries where free-riding problems existed (Pittman 1977, 47–50).[5] Thus, the returns from rent seeking are influenced not only by the level of government involvement in the economy but also by the ability of special interests to free ride on the efforts of others.

The expected returns from political influence must also take into account the social (or deadweight) costs associated with a subsidy or regulation and the taxes required to support it. Gary Becker (1985) has developed a formal model to demonstrate that the social costs of subsidies discourage pressure by subsidized groups and the social costs of taxes encourage pressure by taxed groups. Becker contends that since the *marginal* social costs of subsidies rise (while *marginal* social benefits decline) as subsidies are increased, recipients of subsidies are discouraged from exerting additional pressure as subsidies are increased, even in the absence of any taxpayer reaction. Increased subsidies, and therefore the taxes to support them, encourage taxpayers to exert greater pressure by raising the marginal social cost of taxes. In short, higher subsidies and taxes raise the countervailing political power of taxpayers. Political support withers, then, as the deadweight costs of regulations or subsidies become large. Simply put, an increase in the social costs of taxation encourages pressure by taxpayers because taxpayers are then harmed more by tax payments while an increase in the deadweight cost of subsidies or regulations discourages pressure by the lucky recipients because they now benefit less from the captured subsidies:

> An increase in the marginal deadweight cost of taxes . . . raises the pressure exerted by taxpayers essentially because a reduction in taxes then has a smaller (adverse) effect on the revenue from taxation. On the other hand, an increase in the marginal deadweight cost of subsidies . . . reduces the pressure exerted by recipients because a given increase in the subsidy then requires a larger increase in tax revenue. (Becker 1983, 381)

---

5. Pittman's analysis alerts us to the relevance of industry structure (e.g., size of firms, market share, regulation, number of industries, number of employees, government purchases, leverage) in shaping corporate political involvement. Industry structure determines market performance, not merely through the mechanisms of pricing and production (output) but also by advantaging or disadvantaging certain industries in the competition for political clout. Unfortunately, empirical evidence of a positive relationship between industry structure and corporate PAC (political action committee) contributions remains rather inconclusive. For a discussion of these empirical studies and further analysis of the effects of industry structure, see Grier, Munger, and Roberts 1991.

Becker's observation that the expected returns to special interests are at least in part determined by the countervailing pressure of opposing groups is not novel to political science. In fact, David Truman recognized that the "wavelike" movements of groups in and out of the political sphere were a response to the "need of protection from the activities of economic and political rivals" (1951, 79). The political activities of one group spur the involvement of other groups: "other groups are created to present different claims and to push opposing policies, and, in turn, still other groups grow up in response to these, and so on" (Truman 1951, 79). Truman, however, attributed the wavelike actions of groups to social and economic disturbances—the results of which cannot be effectively dealt with by the groups without governmental mediation and authority—rather than governmental policies relating to taxes and subsidies: "Disturbances growing out of the market cannot all be settled directly by trade associations or monopolistic economic groups. These groups must supplement direct action by making claims through or upon some mediating institutionalized group whose primary characteristic is its wider powers" (1951, 105). In any event, it seems clear that the rate of return that groups can anticipate to result from governmental influence is affected by competition from other groups.[6]

Another factor related to the costs of influence, and therefore the returns from rent seeking, is the price of a political favor. Denzau and Munger (1986) regard the price of a political favor (or policy) as a function of the cost to the legislator of providing the service. This cost, in turn, depends on the productivity of the legislator's effort and the extent to which his or her constituents favor the group's aims or policy. The more adept the legislator is at producing the desired service—due to favorable committee assignments, contacts, seniority, competence,

---

6. Cooperation seems to be the optimal political strategy for special interests, especially when cooperative action can be expected to expand the sum of rents available. However, when a zero-sum game develops so that rent-seeking activities create winners and losers, "war" between rent seekers arises over the fixed rents. One example of this is the relationship between teachers' salaries and welfare spending. For example, Richard Vedder and Lowell Gallaway (1991) found that average teacher salaries were positively related to other forms of government spending when such spending was low (cooperation) but negatively related to other expenditures when such spending was high (competition). Not all rent seeking is competitive, however. One of the problems that Theodore Lowi (1969) sees in "interest-group liberalism" is that instead of competition among special interests, they collude to shape policies benefiting all of the groups involved: "Interest-group liberalism offers a justification for keeping major combatants apart. It provides a theoretical basis for giving to each according to his claim, the price for which is a reduction of concern for what others are claiming. In other words, it transforms logrolling from necessary evil to greater good" (Lowi 1969, 76).

and so on—the lower the price. For example, the committee seat that a legislator "owns" gives him or her a comparative advantage over politicians who are not on the committee in influencing policies within the committee's jurisdiction. This implies that legislators on a committee with jurisdiction over a policy area that concerns an interest group will have a cost advantage in producing services: groups tend to purchase these services from low-cost suppliers through campaign contributions (Endersby and Munger 1992, 83).

The more productive a legislator's efforts on behalf of a group, or the less hostile voters are to the special treatment given a group, the lower the (minimum) price a group must pay. To the extent that voters are both informed and opposed to a policy, a special interest seeking favorable government treatment must pay a higher price than it would if all voters were either indifferent or uninformed. "A legislator seeking reelection must be compensated for votes lost by serving an interest group before he will provide such services. The amount required varies with the distaste of voters for the policy" (Denzau and Munger 1986, 99). This may explain why reinforcing the opinions of group supporters in the legislature is such a dominant concern of interest groups: the costs and risks are less than those incurred in attempting to change the opinion of a legislator already predisposed (perhaps because of constituent opinion) to oppose the group.

Indeed, it would seem that the costs of rent seeking are strongly influenced by whether groups seek to change or reinforce legislator predispositions, with reinforcement costing less. In fact, a large amount of literature on groups suggests that lobbying efforts are aimed at reinforcing those who already agree with a group's positions. Donald Matthews (1973, 191), contends that "lobbying changes relatively few votes. Indeed, not much lobbying is intended to do so. The principal effect of lobbying is not conversion but reinforcement." A more recent analysis of group lobbying in the House of Representative reaches similar conclusions: "groups do tend to lobby their partisan and ideological allies" (Wright 1990, 429). Wright, however, also suggests that legislators "respond and adjust to the balance of group pressures they experience" (1990, 434). Wright observed that voting decisions in both the Ways and Means and Agriculture Committees in the House of Representatives on issues related to group interests were influenced by the number of contacts that committee members had with group representatives, especially those in favor of the legislation. Because of statistical problems in his analysis—multicolinearity between party, ideology, and perhaps constituent economic interests—it is impossible to determine the impact of lobbying relative to the personal predispositions of legislators. Nonetheless, Wright's analysis raises the distinct possibility that conversion may be more prevalent than previously thought, perhaps because conversion is not that "costly" if legislators are relatively uninformed. In that case, any "bit" of information will reduce a legislator's ambivalence or uncertainty and influence his or her decision. This latter premise is supported by Richard Smith's provocative study "Advocacy, Interpretation, and Influence in the U.S. Congress" (1984).

According to Smith, time and cognitive constraints motivate legislators to simplify their decisions thereby forcing them to neglect some of the possible consequences of a policy on their own goal attainment. This occurs for two reasons: first, legislators engage in only a limited search for information about policies; second, some potentially relevant information about the consequences of a policy are ignored because of poor perceptions due, again, to cognitive constraints on human memory and information processing. Therefore, by supplying interpretations of policies, groups produce opinion conversions on the part of legislators. In a real sense, they operate like Anthony Downs's "persuaders": "they provide only those facts which are favorable to whatever group they are supporting . . . . these 'facts' will never be false, but they need not tell the whole truth" (1957, 83). Such presentations influence legislator perceptions by structuring how members search for information, causing legislators to reconsider information that they may have unintentionally ignored in previous searches. "The aim is to show how the position favored by the advocate is also one consistent with the goals of the members—either by shaping the members' personal understandings of the consequences or by providing members with acceptable explanations of their positions" (Smith 1984, 47). Thus, where legislators lack relevant information, the cost of influence is lower for interest groups. This supplies some of the incentive for groups to try to convert legislators to their side, rather than merely reinforcing the preferences of their supporters.

The Relevance of Group Size to Rent Seeking

If there is one variable that has consumed a lot of theorizing by leading economists, it is group or industry size. For instance, George Stigler's (1971, 12) theory of economic regulation views policy as essentially a political auction where the highest bidder receives the right to tax the wealth of others. The costs involved in exploiting the political process to this end account for the frequent success of small groups in regulatory policy, according to Stigler. He argues that since voters must spend resources to become informed about a policy and its impact on their wealth, information costs must offset prospective gains to voters. However, the small per capita stake that most voters stand to gain assures that few (voters) will become sufficiently informed to exercise influence. Therefore, numerically large, diffuse interest groups normally will not be effective bidders for public policies, and small groups will have an inordinate amount of influence. This point is similar to that of Anthony Downs (1957) who suggests that the costs of information compel government to follow the views of the few rather than the many:

> influencers are specialists in whatever policy areas they wish to influence; whereas voters are generalists trying to draw an overall comparison between parties. Specialization demands expert knowledge and information, especially if competition is keen, but most men cannot afford to become expert in many fields simultaneously. Therefore influencers usually operate in only one or two policy areas at once. This means that in each area, only a small number of specialists are trying to influence the government. (254)

Stigler makes another point about group size: the costs of organization set limits on group size, especially with respect to the effectiveness of large groups. For example, effective groups must overcome the familiar free-rider problem that plagues collective efforts to influence legislators and other important politicians. Moreover, as the size of a group expands so does the cost of the transfer to society, thereby intensifying opposition. "Larger industries seek programs which cost the society more and arouse more opposition from substantially affected groups. The tasks of persuasion, both within and without the industry, also increase with size" (Stigler 1971, 12). In short, Stigler suggests that there are some diseconomies of scale associated with large groups and that beyond some point it becomes counterproductive to dilute the per capita wealth transfer by enlarging the size of the group benefiting from the transfer.

Sam Peltzman (1976) expanded Stigler's model by introducing opposition groups as another consideration in determining wealth transfers. For Peltzman, those responsible for determining the transfer—vote-maximizing regulators—trade off the rents given to producers relative to the costs imposed on consumers. For the "regulator," the marginal political return from a transfer (in votes) must equal the marginal political cost of the associated tax. Here again, group size plays an important role in the regulator's decision: "The crucial decision that the regulator (or would-be regulator) must make in this model is the numerical size of the group he favors, and thus implicitly the size of the group he taxes" (Peltzman 1976, 214).

Gary Becker (1983) incorporates Peltzman's notion of opposition groups into his model of group competition for political influence. Becker views groups in the same way as Stigler (1971) and Peltzman (1976): they are dedicated to maximizing the income of their members through governmental action. Competition among these groups for political influence determines the structure of taxes, subsidies, and other favors granted through the political process. Becker considers all political activities that raise the income of a group as subsidies to that group and activities that lower income as taxes. The total amount available for subsidies equals the total amount raised through taxes by assumption (1983, 372). Groups compete for political influence by spending time, energy, and money on the production of political pressure. Since free riding raises the costs of producing pressure, expenditures on the production of pressure must include expenditures on direct political action as well as expenditures to control free riding (e.g., policing behavior, reducing the incentives to shirk through cost-sharing mechanisms). The more efficient a special interest is at producing political pressure, the higher its subsidy or the lower its taxes. Hence, greater control over free riding raises the optimal pressure by a group and thereby increases its subsidy or reduces its taxes. This premise predicts that smaller groups will have an advantage in the competition for political influence since free riding is usually more easily controlled in small groups.

Becker also sees competition among groups as influenced by the deadweight costs of taxes and subsidies. Here too, group size plays a significant role in his theory: "Since deadweight costs to taxpayers fall as the tax per person falls, the opposition of taxpayers to subsidies decreases as the number of taxpayers increases. Therefore, groups can more readily obtain subsidies when they are small relative to the number of taxpayers" (1983, 395). Small groups may suffer in their competition with larger ones, however, if larger groups can take advantage of scale economies in the production of pressure—another factor determining the efficiency of a group in producing political pressure.

Richard Posner (1974), drawing upon the theory of cartels, also emphasizes the importance of size to the success of groups in obtaining political favors, particularly economic regulations. The theory of cartels implies that the difficulty in getting individuals (firms, groups, industries) to cooperate in maintaining a monopoly price is most likely to be overcome if the number of "sellers" whose actions must be coordinated is small. This reduces the costs of coordination and policing. Similarly, the fewer the prospective beneficiaries, the easier it will be for them to coordinate their efforts to obtain political favors and the more difficult for any one of them to refuse to contribute to the maintenance of the monopoly. Likewise, the smaller the group, the more homogeneous the interests of the group and the easier it will be for them "to arrive at a common position and the more likely it will be that the common position does not disadvantage one or more members as to cause them to defect from the group" (Posner 1974, 345). Clearly, then, the size of interest groups affects their ability to mobilize supporters and to obtain the resources necessary to influence government. This relationship is central to Mancur Olson's (1965) classic study, *The Logic of Collective Action*.

Olson contends that both the likelihood of approaching optimality in the supply of a collective good, such as lobbying the legislature for preferential treatment, and the probability of constraining free-rider tendencies decrease as the size of a group increases. This premise is based upon the following line of argument:

> First, the larger the group, the smaller the fraction of the total group benefit any person acting in the group interest receives, and the less adequate the reward for any group-oriented action, and the farther the group falls short of getting an optimal supply of the collective good, even if it should get some. Second, since the larger the group, the smaller the share of total benefit going to any individual, or to any (absolutely) small subset of members of the group, the less the likelihood that any small subset of the group, much less any single individual, will gain enough for getting the collective good to bear the burden of providing even a small amount of it; in other words, the larger the group, the smaller the likelihood of oligopolistic interaction that might help obtain the good. Third, the larger the number of members in the group, the greater the organization costs, and thus the higher the hurdle that must be jumped before any of the collective good at all can be obtained. (Olson 1965, 48)

Thus, small ("privileged") groups, according to Olson, are better able to mobilize resources to influence government. Large groups, in contrast, are plagued by free-rider problems. In fact, only through coercion or the use of selective (private good) incentives are large groups able to supply themselves with meaningful amounts of valued collective goods. Since one's reward, as well as effort, is imperceptible in large groups and once the collective good is supplied no group member can be prohibited from consuming its benefits, rational action in large groups dictates shirking—free riding. This leads Olson to suggest that the lobbying activities of large special interests are a by-product of the operation of selective incentives—they have nothing to do with why members initially join the group but are made possible *because* members join.

The Impact of Special Interest Money

The influence of special interest money (PAC contributions) and lobbying on Congress ranges from little to insignificant, according to many (if not most) studies of group influence. Even when significant effects can be uncovered, a legislator's party affiliation, ideological views, and the economic interests of constituents seem to be far more important in determining roll-call behavior. William Welch (1980), for instance, examined the effects of 1974 PAC contributions by dairy interests on the following year's congressional vote on price supports for milk. While he concluded that the dairy PACs had rewarded legislators for their support, he found that PAC money had a relatively small effect on the vote: the positions of members of Congress were largely explained by party, ideology, and the significance of dairy production in each legislator's constituency. Similarly, Henry Chappell (1982) found a significant positive relationship between PAC money and legislative voting but only on one of the several bills he examined. Likewise, Diana Evans (1986) found a marginal influence for PAC money on two important rent-seeking legislative measures: the Chrysler loan guarantee and the windfall profits oil tax. PAC contributions were among the least important factors in roll-call votes on these issues: "Finally, lest the point be lost in the glare of the spotlight on PAC contributions, it is still true that in most cases PAC money has less effect on members' voting than their partisan and ideological persuasions" (Evans 1986, 127). Members of Congress seem to follow their partisan and ideological leanings far more than the trail of PAC cash.

John Wright (1985) examined the campaign contributions from five major PACs that were both large and legislatively active on roll-call decisions in the Ninety-seventh Congress. Wright, too, concluded that in none of the five cases were campaign contributions important enough to change the legislative outcomes from what they would have been in the absence of contributions: "For example, if the auto dealers had made no contributions in 1979–1980, then, on average, each congressman's probability of voting to overturn the FTC regulation on used cars would have been lowered by .019 (e.g., from a .6 probability of supporting the NADA to a probability of support of .581). Clearly, the changes . . . are rather paltry" (1985, 411). Moreover, "campaign contributions exhibited little effect on voting decisions once organized lobbying efforts were taken into account" (Wright 1990, 431).

Some studies fail to uncover even a chemical trace of the influence of special interest money on congressional voting. For instance, Janet Grenzke (1989), in one of the most thorough longitudinal analyses of PAC contributions and legislative voting, found that "contributions from 120 PACs affiliated with 10 large interest groups generally do not maintain or change House members' voting patterns" (1989, 19). Grenzke first examined the hypothesis that members vote in a pro-PAC manner because they receive larger contributions than others, but she found little evidence to support this hypothesis (6–13). She then explored the possibility that *changes in PAC contributions* bring about changes in the voting behavior of members of Congress. Again, Grenzke found little evidence of such an effect (14–18). Both of these conclusions were bolstered by her personal interviews with PAC officials.

Such findings may make us far too sanguine about group involvement in politics. The lack of strong statistical evidence of influence can lead to the easy conclusion that group pressure is of marginal significance.[7] There is, however, another explanation for the lack of strong empirical relationships. One reason for the minimal effects of special interest money, and perhaps lobbying, is the leverage that legislators command in the "market" for special interest contributions. Examination of the structure of the market in which PAC contributions change hands suggests that leverage in such markets is frequently with the sellers (politicians, legislators). First, the number of buyers—PACs—exceeds the number of sellers in the market. In such a market there are hundreds of PACs but only two sellers (the incumbent politician and the challenger) in most congressional races. In addition, from the perspective of PACs there are no close substitutes for a particular incumbent politician's seniority, experience, or contacts in Washington. Third, since it is very difficult for a challenger to defeat an incumbent, entry barriers are quite high. These conditions characterize a seller's market. Although PACs could collude by coordinating their contributions to reduce the leverage of politicians, a large number of buyers relative to the number of sellers, readily available substitutes on the buyers' side (other PACs) but not on the sellers' side, and entry barriers confronting sellers suggest that most of the leverage is on the side of the politician (Keim and Zardkoohi 1988). From this perspective, special interest

---

7. Gordon Tullock has pointed out that it is virtually impossible to evaluate the effectiveness of groups or the exact payoff of various lobbying activities because "commonly they are interested not in the whole bill but in some minor clause in it. They may get that taken care of" (personal correspondence, May 1993). Tullock's point is well taken: buried within a lengthy legislative measure, such provisions escape the notice of most legislators and are frequently passed with little or no fanfare.

money may lack substantial influence because politicians rule that market and make choices as to which groups to favor on the basis of other considerations (e.g., ideology) rather than merely on the amount of money offered. If this is true, politicians may be obtaining rents for assisting groups that they are already predisposed to favor. Since rational politicians have no incentive to reveal their policy preferences, groups probably pay more than they need to in order to influence the behavior of such politicians.

Summary

The study of groups and their influence on public policy can be subsumed within the economic paradigm termed *rent seeking*. Rent seeking involves the actions of groups to obtain artificially contrived transfers of wealth through the political process. Groups hope to obtain significant returns in terms of economic rents—profits in excess of opportunity costs. Groups desire direct subsidies, barriers to the entry of rivals, control over policies affecting substitutes and complements to group outputs, and price-fixing policies beneficial to the special interest. In the pursuit of these objectives, interest groups seek access to decision makers, the election of "friendly" legislators, votes on specific legislation, bureaucratic favors, and protection from others seeking to reduce or eliminate preferential treatment. In obtaining these goals, groups are prepared to "buy" favorable legislation, with the cost including the price of the service and organizational expenses. One important influence on the returns to groups is size: small groups may have an advantage in organizing for political action. Hence, there are some notable diseconomies of scale associated with large groups (e.g., consumers) that prevents them from bidding effectively for governmental policy.

CHAPTER 2

A Model for Studying Adverse Selection

In this chapter, I describe the analytic tools I use in exploring the evolution of Congress within a rent-seeking society. Many of the issues raised here are elaborated upon in the following chapters. The basic model that guides this inquiry incorporates four assumptions:

1. Legislators, and those seeking to become legislators, are rational utility-maximizers
2. Long service in politics reflects one's preference for the intrinsic, rather than the material, rewards of public service
3. The intrinsic returns to officeholding accrue value with tenure in the job, all things being equal
4. Rent-seeking behavior in a legislature reduces the intrinsic returns to a legislative career

The first assumption is the central premise of rational choice analysis—namely, that individuals seek the greatest benefit from their actions. To this basic assumption I add three more to represent the impact of a rent-seeking society on legislative institutions. The underlying premise for these assumptions is that both intrinsic and material returns are available through legislative service, but rent seeking furthers material rewards at the expense of intrinsic ones. *Intrinsic returns* serves as a "hypothetical construct" or a "theoretical term" that relates the rewards of public service to legislator behavior and the organization of Congress. "Its meaning derives from the part that it plays in the whole theory in which it is embedded, and from the role of the theory itself" (Kaplan 1964, 56). In this sense, it serves the same function as other explanatory terms like *attitudes* and *power*. The use of this construct yields insights about institutional service, and the external costs (externalities) associated with such service, that have gone largely unnoticed. Although the intrinsic returns to public office might be assessed by determining the level of satisfaction derived from various legislative activities (e.g., creating legislation) and experiences (e.g., exercising power), there is no reason to expect rational politicians to reveal their true preferences for these rewards any more than they would reveal their true preferences for financial gain. Thus, we will have to look at the behavior of politicians for unobtrusive clues as to their preferences for intrinsic rather than financial rewards.

Intrinsic Returns and Assumptions in the Model

While perhaps not a major motivating force in some important forms of congressional behavior (e.g., roll-call voting), the intrinsic returns of legislative service are significant for two reasons: they are available on a *daily basis* and can be consumed in large amounts without paying the costs associated with the supply—that is, a collective good. The day-to-day activities of legislators entail significant personal costs—meeting with constituents, handling requests for constituent service, listening to debate and committee deliberations, grappling with intractable social problems to name a few—that can be avoided only at great peril. Legislative achievements normally are too sporadic to sustain the high level of commitment to public service required of legislators on a daily basis. Aside from pay, the only rewards available to legislators on a daily basis are intrinsic ones. Hence, I suspect that the intrinsic returns from legislative service sustain many of the day-to-day sacrifices and activities of legislators. These features, along with the assumption that intrinsic returns accrue value with seniority, make the intrinsic returns from congressional service an important consumption activity of legislators.

It is almost impossible to find substantial empirical evidence that legislators, or prospective legislators, seek financial gain or the extra legislative pay resulting from congressional service (see, for example, Jacobson 1990; Canon 1990; Craig 1993). The relevance of intrinsic returns to the motivations for public service has fared no better in terms of empirical support. If material or intrinsic returns are so important, why have we found so little evidence of their existence in candidates' expressed motivations for congressional service? Studies of why individuals pursue political office have placed considerable reliance upon interviews with prospective or incumbent legislators. Perhaps some preferences can be uncovered through interviews (e.g., career and family experiences), but others may be far more difficult to measure through personal interviews because the questions are highly reactive and potentially embarrassing. Economists have been acutely aware of this problem—namely, that rational politicians have no incentive to *reveal their true preferences*.

Clearly, there are socially acceptable answers to most survey queries, and it does not take a great leap of faith to expect politicians to be aware of this fact when they answer questions. This is not to disparage what we have learned at the hands of skilled interviewers and through elite interviews. My point is that some questions cannot be addressed through most elite interviews no matter how noble the objectives of the survey, skillful the interviewer, or valid the promise of complete anonymity. If a politician were even to publicly mention an interest in financial gain (e.g., salary), or a desire to consume the nonmaterial benefits of service in an elite institution, he or she might have a very short career in politics. We expect our politicians to sacrifice for the public good and to enjoy doing so. Politicians should never seek office because they enjoy the deference and power associated with elite status; to do so would be to admit to arrogance and self-indulgence. In sum, previous empirical research on the preferences and goals of politicians seeking legislative office probably underestimates the relevance of both material and intrinsic returns simply because of the difficulty in determining true preferences.

Intrinsic returns can be viewed as encompassing the satisfaction that derives from the on-the-job consumption of such things as importance of the position, public admiration and respect for the office, national visibility, influence, power, and public service. Long service in politics is construed as evidence of one's preference for these (intrinsic) returns. There are two reasons why long careers in politics serve as evidence of preferences for the intrinsic returns of a congressional career (assumption 2). First, the legal compensation associated with public service is normally less than could be obtained through a similar level of executive employment in the private sector. Comparisons of legislator salaries with those available in the private sector are a common feature of efforts (even by independent commissions) to raise legislative compensation, and the arguments are quite persuasive: public service entails financial sacrifices, at least in terms of explicit salary (see, for example, Matlack and Caspar 1989): "Even if we look only at non-profit institutions and organizations, which provide psychic satisfactions similar to high federal offices, the salaries paid to high-level officers of major non-profit institutions such as universities, hospitals, and large cultural centers, generally are well above those paid in top levels of government" (Report of the 1989 Commission on Executive, Legislative and Judicial Salaries 1988, 15).

In fact, executive-level salaries in the private sector have actually increased in constant dollars since 1969 while the salaries of legislators (in constant dollars) have declined sharply (Report of the 1989 Commission on Executive, Legislative and Judicial Salaries 1988, 17, chart 5). While recent increases in the congressional salary might seem substantial, annual wages and military pay grew at a greater rate: the congressional salary in 1992 was about 300 percent greater than the salary in

1969, but the average annual wage increased by 385 percent, and military pay increased by 401 percent (Merck 1993). Thus, a long career of public service can be construed as reflecting one's preference for the intrinsic rather than the material rewards of public service; otherwise, one would exit public office for the more lucrative financial returns associated with employment in the private sector. As one senior legislator remarked about the rewards of serving in Congress:

> Of course members aren't being paid enough. You can't pay members of Congress in proportion to the importance of the position. A large part of the compensation *has* to come in the satisfaction of doing the job—the intangibles of holding office, making good policy and serving the country. (Hibbing 1982a, 67)

Second, even if the flow of extralegal pay encouraged members to remain in Congress, legislators interested in maximizing their wealth would still have short careers in Congress: ethics laws and financial disclosure rules have the capacity to illuminate legislator wrongdoings, and the longer a legislator is involved in favor selling the greater the risk of being found out and punished. Given these risks, those interested in gaining financially from congressional service would seem to prosper most when they leave office; only then can they escape the institutional and public scrutiny associated with monetary gain. This may explain why a congressional study (House 1977a, 433) reported that retiring legislators increased their salary in their first job after leaving Congress by an average of over 50 percent! Moreover, the longer legislators wait to leave Congress, the greater the probability that special interests will discount the value of the services rendered ("what have you done for me lately" is a refrain appropriate to interest groups as well as legislators). In short, I assume that potential congressional recruits, as well as those presently members of the legislature, *reveal their preferences* for the intrinsic returns of congressional service by establishing long careers in politics, thereby foregoing the financial gain of private-sector employment.

As legislators gain tenure, their political influence also rises and they are in a better position to enjoy the intrinsic returns of legislative service. For instance, rising tenure increases the likelihood of obtaining a formal position of leadership (e.g., subcommittee or committee leader), gaining national visibility as an expert, being recognized as a dedicated public servant, and perhaps even influencing the content of major legislation. Thus, the intrinsic returns to legislators increase the longer they remain in office, all things being equal (assumption 3). This proviso to the third assumption is necessary because of the last assumption: rent-seeking behavior within a legislature reduces the intrinsic returns to a legislative career.

There are at least two ways in which rent-seeking behavior reduces the intrinsic returns that accumulate with legislative service (assumption 4). First, rent-seeking behavior reduces the esteem of the institution in the eyes of its citizens. Instead of being perceived as dedicated public servants, members of a rent-seeking legislature are viewed as self-interested and out for financial gain; perceptions of corruption and questions about ethics haunt all who serve in the institution. Clearly, service in an institution that lacks public respect and the dogged pursuit of a legislative career that generates suspicion rather than acclaim are investments with small intrinsic returns. In short, public disapprobation of its institutions reduces the intrinsic returns that are associated with careers in those institutions.

Second, rent-seeking behavior in a legislature forces even those disinclined to engage in such behavior to do so just to protect the interests of their constituencies or to assure a competitive position for district producers. As one set of groups obtains preferential treatment, another set of groups seeks either protection from the legislative action taken on behalf of competing groups or legislative action granting them special exemptions. And candidates proposing to eliminate rent seeking may never get elected! Amihai Glazer persuasively argues that "when one candidate is expected to consider campaign contributions when he awards contracts, whereas the other candidate promises to avoid rent seeking, then the latter candidate will receive no contributions, and will lose the election. The result holds even though the firms prefer that there be no rent-seeking" (1993, 14). Thus, even those who value a congressional career and the intrinsic returns it provides engage in rent seeking to counter the efforts of others to obtain preferential treatment for their constituency interests. Hence, all members in the institution are "forced" to engage in some degree of defensive (or "protective") rent seeking. This further reduces the incentives to expose the practice to public notice or legislative investigation thereby stifling reforms designed to constrain rent-seeking behavior.

Many legislators probably dislike rent-seeking activities but all find it essential to perform these duties; if they don't perform these activities, they may find themselves saddled with well-financed opposition at the next election. And congressmen must also forget about excusing themselves from helping district interests through the political process on the argument that it raises an already large budget deficit. Many constituents couldn't care less about the impact of pork-barreling on the budget. For example, a 1991 opinion survey of Floridians (Survey Research

Laboratory, Florida State University) found wide approval for pork-barreling: 88 percent of those interviewed felt that it was "very" or "somewhat" important for their representative to "bring money to the district"; 60 percent of those who felt pork-barreling was important acknowledged that such district largesse increased the deficit, and about one half of these respondents willingly admitted that it raised the deficit by at least a moderate amount. Constituents, apparently, approve of their legislators' helping district interests through the political process, even if it adds significantly to an already existing budget deficit! Admittedly, there is more than a little irony in the fact that constituents want their legislators to "bring home the bacon" but abhor the rent-seeking activity that often arises in serving district interests. If legislators ever need a justification for engaging in rent-seeking behavior, serving constituency interests is a rationalization that is readily accepted by district voters.[1]

The need to engage in some form of rent seeking to obtain needed campaign funds or to avoid questions of responsiveness to district needs diminishes the intrinsic returns to officeholding by forcing members to devote scarce resources to rent seeking. For instance, if a legislator becomes the leader of a subcommittee, he or she can enjoy the benefits that are associated with expertise and influence, but that position of influence also puts the leader in closer contact with groups and fellow legislators engaged in rent seeking. This requires the subcommittee leader to allocate resources for dealing with the rent-seeking demands of one's colleagues thereby diminishing the time and resources devoted to more rewarding activities (e.g., drafting legislation). Thus, legislators find the job of "errand boy" rather demeaning and costly, which detracts from the intrinsic returns of a legislative career.

Former legislators who retire from office claiming the job has changed—become more difficult or less rewarding—can be viewed as leaving office because of declining intrinsic returns. I suspect that the level of rent seeking in the legislature directly or indirectly has a lot to do

---

1. I should also point out that rent seeking may be construed broadly as "constituency service" in the sense that a legislator's efforts to obtain favorable treatment for constituency interests is often characterized as such. These activities can be differentiated on the basis of the returns to legislators: if a legislator exacts a price for his or her service, either in the form of quasilegal (e.g., campaign contributions, honoraria) or illegal pay, rent seeking occurs. If, on the other hand, serving constituents' interests involves no further remuneration—that is, it is part of the representational contract between agent and principal—and no favorable fiscal treatment transpires (i.e., use of the political process to obtain rent-earning regulations or legislation), the service is not construed as rent seeking.

with these retirement decisions. Rent-seeking behavior directly reduces the intrinsic returns to officeholding by requiring legislators to devote resources to that activity to remain in office or to protect district interests and indirectly diminishes these returns by lowering the esteem of the institution and all who serve within it. For these reasons, I assume that rent seeking reduces the intrinsic returns to institutional service.

Adverse Selection Hypotheses

These four assumptions generate four testable hypotheses that relate to the problem of adverse selection in a rent-seeking society:

1. The intrinsic returns from office holding are reduced by rent-seeking activity in a legislature to the point that individuals with the highest regard for these (intrinsic) rewards enter Congress in decreased proportions, thereby leaving the institution to those preferring financial rewards
2. Rent seekers manipulate institutional arrangements to promote wealth-earning opportunities, often precipitating scandals
3. Newer generations of legislators engage in rent-seeking activity to a greater extent than do earlier cohorts
4. Declines in the intrinsic returns of a congressional career result in the exodus of those who gain the most from these rewards (i.e., career politicians)

These hypotheses were derived in the following manner. By assumption 4, rent-seeking behavior reduces the intrinsic returns to legislative service; hence, we might expect individuals with expressed preferences for the intrinsic rather than the material rewards of public service to seek other career options. If rent seeking reduces the intrinsic returns to officeholding, then those drawn to office for these reasons will decline as a proportion of entering cohorts (hypothesis 1). Since long service in politics is evidence of one's preference for the intrinsic over the material rewards of officeholding (assumption 2), we can expect career politicians to be less prevalent among entering congressional cohorts. This results in a candidate pool that is comprised of individuals without an expressed commitment to public service thereby enhancing the prospect for rent-seeking behavior. Maximizing utility (assumption 1) for rent seekers entails the accumulation of wealth; the political process and institutional arrangements can be manipulated and exploited to this end (hypothesis 2). As a result, rent seekers frequently engage in the types of behavior that precipitate public outrage when uncovered.

While all legislators find it necessary to engage in some degree of rent seeking to defend constituency interests from time to time, more recent generations may reveal a greater appetite for these activities. Since the intrinsic returns from officeholding are likely to be small for most low-tenure legislators, and discounted further because of the declining popular esteem of Congress (Parker 1989), rent seeking will be a more attractive activity than the consumption of the intrinsic rewards of officeholding for recent generations of legislators (hypothesis 3). Thus increases in rent-seeking behavior over time may be at least partially a function of generational changes in the composition of Congress: the entry of politicians drawn to legislative service less by their interest in the intrinsic returns from congressional service and more by the rewards associated with rent-seeking.

As the intrinsic returns to officeholding decline with increased rent-seeking activity inside the legislature (assumption 4), we can expect that those officials who gain their greatest utility from these rewards—namely, career legislators (assumption 3)—will exit the institution for more rewarding work. Thus, the diminished value of a congressional career, resulting from the rent-seeking demands placed upon willing and unwilling legislators alike, results in the retirement of career legislators (hypothesis 4).

I have suggested that long service in political office can be construed as revealing one's preference for the intrinsic rather than the material returns to officeholding (assumption 2). This is one reason why career politicians are less likely to engage in practices designed to increase wealth. There is another asset to career politicians that reduces the likelihood of rent-seeking behavior in Congress: their sizable career investments. Unlike career politicians, "amateurs" are less constrained by risks to reputational capital since they have less invested in their political careers. Politicians, by investing time and effort into their political careers, incur sunk costs that are capitalized into their reputations (brand names). This creates incentives for career politicians to protect their investments by avoiding unethical behavior that might, if uncovered, damage their reputations. Political novices, in contrast, have not yet made the same level of investment as career politicians; hence, they have incurred fewer sunk costs. Therefore, noncareer politicians have less invested in their careers and stand to lose less if those careers come to a premature end because malfeasance in office is uncovered. The low level of sunk costs invested by amateurs in their political careers means that the gains from unethical behavior will almost always exceed their career investments. Hence, the cost of engaging in unethical behavior is a lot higher for career politicians than for amateurs. Simply put, from the standpoint of voters who fear corruption of public officials, noncareer politicians entail considerable risk.

It can be persuasively argued that political amateurs do not constitute a homogeneous class of politicians. For example, David Canon (1990) has described three "ideal" types of amateur politicians: "ambitious" amateurs who have personalities and ambitions similar to those of experienced politicians who pursue careers in politics; "policy" amateurs who are interested in advocating and shaping public policy; and "hopeless" amateurs who run for office to fill the party's ticket or because they enjoy the thrill of political campaigning. For the purposes of this inquiry, the career horizon of a politician is the critical factor in distinguishing between career and noncareer politicians. Career politicians are committed to pursuing long careers in public service; noncareer politicians have no long-term interest in a career in public service—they have distinctly limited career horizons. The notion of limited career horizons is evident in many discussions of amateur politicians. It fits Canon's characterization of the "hopeless amateur" and Barber's description of the "Advertiser": "All things considered, it seems unlikely that the Advertiser will stay very long in the legislature. His original intention is to serve a short hitch and move on" (1965, 115). This attribute—limited interest in establishing a career in politics—is an important difference between career and noncareer politicians. While all noncareer politicians can be described as "amateurs," not all amateurs are noncareer politicians. The term amateur is used in this inquiry to denote noncareer politicians, not novices embarking on what they hope is a long career in politics.

As noted earlier, some amateurs may have made a career out of seeking and contesting public office. In these instances, the motivations to establish a political career are present but success is lacking. I am not bothered by the entrance of amateurs who aspire to establish long legislative careers, but I am troubled by those who enter Congress without such career commitments. Since the intrinsic returns of congressional service gain value with tenure, they are likely to be discounted at a higher rate, or even minimized, by legislators who do not value long political careers. Yet, the intrinsic returns of public service serve as important constraints on rent-seeking activity. Intrinsic returns gain value with tenure (assumption 3) so that even long-time rent seekers eventually gain a greater appreciation for the intrinsic returns of officeholding *with time*. The attraction of the intrinsic rewards to a congressional career increases as legislators gain tenure and, therefore, greater access to positions of influence and prominence. Intrinsic returns also gain attraction because the returns from rent seeking can be expected to eventually decline.

The Production of Rents

If we view rent-seeking activities (e.g., interceding in the creation of regulations or other bureaucratic decisions) as creating goods or services that others will purchase, then the basic principles of the economic theory of production should apply. One principle in particular seems relevant to the production of rents: the law of *diminishing marginal product*. Formally, this law implies that as the number of units of (variable) input increases, other inputs held constant, the marginal product of the input declines after a point. In short, increased effort at rent seeking will increase rents, but, after some point, the marginal gain from that effort will yield diminishing and eventually negative returns.

Thus, all legislators can be expected to obtain (material) returns from their rent-seeking efforts by increasing the production of rents. However, the marginal product produced by these efforts should decline after a point so that additional rent-seeking effort produces progressively fewer rewards. As legislators invest more time and effort in rent seeking, they devote less time to other responsibilities. This might result in the neglect of activities that are essential to remaining in office (constituency service, for example) or gaining influence (e.g., meeting with fellow legislators to formulate laws, attending committee meetings, helping other legislators pass their "pet projects"). If a legislator fails to attend to these duties he or she may lose the favor of voters, colleagues, and influential party leaders. This is likely to increase the costs of serving special interests and therefore reduce the returns from rent seeking. For example, neglect of constituency responsibilities may necessitate large doses of campaign money to convince voters to reelect incumbents who have devoted their efforts to assisting special interests rather than constituency service. Hence, the prices these legislators charge for their services are likely to rise (see, for instance, Denzau and Munger 1986). Price increases reduce the demand for service on the part of special interests, thereby lowering the actual returns that rent-seeking legislators receive. Neglect of institutional responsibilities ("shirking") also incurs the wrath of party leaders and therefore raises the costs of gaining their assistance, which is normally essential for the passage of legislation. This also reduces the net value of the rents obtained. In the extreme case where legislators have totally neglected their institutional responsibilities, party leaders may impose prohibitive costs on the rent-seeking efforts of legislators (e.g., preventing legislation from reaching the floor for a vote) so that the total production of rents actually declines despite the increased effort devoted to rent seeking.

Intrinsic returns, therefore, gain attraction because of the growth in these returns with time and the declining productivity of rent-seeking efforts. These relationships are illustrated more formally in figure 2. In this figure, the relationship between individual effort aimed at generating rents and the actual production of rents is illustrated in terms of the economic theory of production. The marginal product (rents) created by increasing the effort devoted to rent-seeking activities experiences a decline after point A, the point of the maximum rate of increase. The total production of rents, however, continues to rise despite the declining marginal productivity of additional efforts at rent seeking. The rate of increase in the total production of rents progressively slows after reaching the maximum point (A'). Total product declines after B', and marginal product becomes negative at the same point (B). Thus, the pay-off from increased rent seeking should eventually decline thereby making the intrinsic returns from officeholding even more attractive. If, however, the intrinsic returns should experience a decline, perhaps due to a loss in institutional esteem, then the ability of seniority to constrain rent seeking is diminished. Thus, legislators can be expected to increase their rent-seeking activity until the value of the intrinsic rewards sacrificed is greater than the utility obtained through greater rent-seeking effort. Institutional conditions—public esteem and the level of rent seeking—affect these intrinsic returns. Hence, when Congress is unpopular and high levels of rent seeking characterize legislative activity intrinsic returns must be heavily discounted in determining the value of the rewards sacrificed.

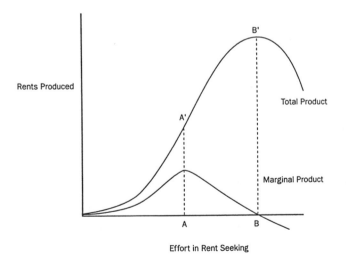

Fig. 2. Diminishing marginal productivity of rent seeking

One final point: since the salaries for public officials are rarely competitive with those earned by elites in the private sector, economists have suggested that these salaries are supplemented with extralegal pay (e.g., rents, campaign contributions). Such salary supplements would make the job worth the sizable investment (e.g., campaign costs) that obtaining congressional office requires. It is hard to dismiss the large number of wealth-generating opportunities available to politicians, but it is equally hard to ignore the intrinsic benefits to legislative office: power, prestige, national prominence, and respect. In short, the difference between the congressional salary and the resources (and effort) required to obtain congressional office reflects not only the potential for extralegislative pay but also the intrinsic returns associated with a congressional career.

Summary

To summarize, adverse selection implies that an increase over time in the number of rent seekers entering Congress drives out those who prefer the intrinsic rewards associated with a legislative career by reducing the esteem of the institution and forcing numbers of Congress to devote resources to rent-seeking activity to counter the efforts of others and to protect constituency interests. As a result, those legislators who gain the most from intrinsic rewards (i.e., those with long tenure in Congress, since intrinsic returns are a function of longevity in office) exit. As Congress becomes populated by rent-seeking legislators, through both recruitment and attrition, institutional rules and arrangements are manipulated to facilitate wealth-earning opportunities. Rent-seeking activity increases further.

If adverse selection is afflicting our political institutions, the market for politicians may come to resemble George Aklerof's characterization of the market for used cars in the United States—a market for "lemons." Simply put, if politicians who prefer intrinsic returns to financial returns shun legislative office, the pool of candidates available for public office will be increasingly composed of those who are either indifferent between intrinsic and material returns or who prefer financial gain to the consumption of the intrinsic rewards to public service. In both cases, the draw of rent seeking looms large.

In the following four chapters, each of the adverse selection hypotheses I have described will be subjected to empirical study: rent seekers manipulate institutional arrangements for financial gain thereby precipitating scandals; rent seeking reduces the attraction of congressional service for those who value the intrinsic returns to officeholding;

increases in rent-seeking behavior are at least partially a response to generational changes in the type of politician entering Congress; and rent seeking hastens the retirement of career legislators. If the symptoms of adverse selection are surfacing, I expect to find empirical support for most, if not all, of these propositions. The reader should be forewarned that the data are not without important caveats, and the derived generalizations will always have explicit or implicit conditions attached to them. This is an exploratory study, and as such it suffers from all of the weaknesses associated with framing new questions for empirical study. I beg the reader's indulgence.

CHAPTER 3

Rent Seeking and Congressional Scandals

In recent years Congress has been rocked—and the public deluged—by one scandal after another. Reports about the selling and buying of political favors, while never suggesting that corruption is a congressional pasttime, seem to plague the institution. While there are numerous causes for the emergence of scandals, some of which are probably idiosyncratic, too little attention has been given to the relevance of rent seeking even though casual observation suggests that rent-seeking behavior is somehow linked to some of Congress's most prominent scandals. For example, "Koreagate" was the term attached to the efforts of a South Korean businessman, Tongsun Park, to influence legislators through illegal gifts and campaign contributions. Park, in turn, collected large commissions from government programs that sold U.S. rice to Korea. The "Wedtec" scandal involved bribing legislators to obtain no-bid contracts. Charles Keating, a rich and influential figure in the thrift industry, bribed senators to pressure regulators to withdraw their efforts to scrutinize and limit the risky investment strategies of the soon-to-be-defunct Lincoln Savings and Loan Association that he owned. The senators and the scandal became known as the "Keating Five."[1]

---

1. A persuasive argument can be made that bribery involves only a transfer of wealth and therefore does not qualify as rent-seeking activity: "A bribe is a transfer, and as such, it represents a method of influencing governmental behavior that does not involve explicit rent-seeking costs. Recall that rent seeking involves the expenditure of costly resources to procure a transfer. Hiring a lawyer or a lobbyist to obtain a favorable law is rent seeking; bribing a legislator for the same law is not" (Tollison 1993, 4). I have no quarrel with this distinction, but it seems overly rigid since both attempts to obtain the law (i.e., hiring a lawyer and bribing a legislator) involve an unnecessary expenditure of resources. Moreover, what if the lawyer hired to obtain a law must resort to bribery? Then the costs of rent seeking clearly involve the unnecessary expenditures involved in hiring the lawyer and bribing the legislator. In addition, it could be argued that legislators overspend to obtain political office, and the bribes associated with officeholding form a large part of the inducement to do so. Hence, bribes also lead to unnecessary expenditures of resources, in this case, overspending to obtain congressional office. For these reasons, I ignore the issue of whether rent seeking involves bribery or a more legal or quasi-legal expenditure of resources. I simply regard rent seeking as involving the socially costly exploitation of the political process to obtain or deliver preferential economic treatment.

While sex scandals involving young clerks and pages have become far more commonplace than in the past, financial gain continues to underlie notable congressional scandals. Whatever the scandal—political stings like Abscam, the selling of votes as in the savings and loan scandal, or the trading of postage stamps for cash—each successive exposé does further damage to Congress's already fragile public image. For example, 77 percent of those surveyed in 1992 believed that legislators wrote "bad checks" at the House bank because "they knew they could get away with it" and 72 percent believed the practice represented "business as usual in Congress" (*American Enterprise* 1992, 84). Even internal congressional "service" organizations, like the House bank and restaurant, appear to be easily corrupted: restaurant bills were left unpaid by exiting legislators, and many present and former legislators "kited" checks at the House bank.

Congress does not energetically pursue reforms, but public outrage can precipitate legislative action to modify or eliminate the scandalized institutional arrangement. The remedies introduced often entail a greater explicitness in the design of institutional rules or the elimination of arrangements subject to exploitation. Are these alterations of institutional arrangements sufficient to eliminate opportunistic behavior in the legislative process? Are we perhaps altering institutional rules without really remedying the problem?

This is not to argue that institutional arrangements, like the patronage system, never invite abuse; however, are any institutional arrangements immune to manipulation? Simply put, legislators bent on financial gain can find ingenious ways to exploit any and all institutional arrangements. If so, then the problem may involve the composition of Congress, in addition to the nature of institutional rules and structures. Both factors may underlie legislative scandals to some degree, but most scholarly and journalistic attention has been given to the structural side of the problem—devious institutional arrangements and rules. We cannot, however, ignore the obvious fact that most scandals would not arise without the collaboration and participation of politicians intent upon enhancing their own personal wealth, either in exploiting (or creating) the scandalized institutional arrangement themselves or refusing to expose or deal harshly with those who do.

The possibility that the type of politician coming to Congress may be more inclined to engage in rent-seeking behavior has been ignored in discussions of the causes of scandals. Instead an effort has been made to equate unethical behavior to the temptation of financial gain. Legislators are not to blame for taking bribes; the culprits are those who offered the bribes! The conventional argument is that "there are always some persons or groups willing to offer bribes or illegal campaign gifts to influence the outcome of legislation, obtain federal contracts, or persuade regulators to look the other way. As a result, numerous senators or representatives have taken bribes or accepted gifts. . . ." (Congressional Quarterly 1992, 51). I am not persuaded that it is solely the combination of temptation and human weakness for financial gain that produce rent-seeking scandals and turn "good" legislators into "bad" ones. Many legislators have resisted such enticements. For example, a large number of representatives and senators have refused honoraria, and others have turned away unusually large bribes, as the Abscam investigation demonstrated.

How, then, do we prevent rent-seeking scandals from arising? We can envision two solutions: prevent special interests from tempting legislators with financial gain or attract politicians to public service who are difficult, if not impossible, to corrupt. Most reforms have concentrated on the first option by regulating contributions, gifts, and outside income and by requiring various types of financial disclosure. Too little consideration has been given to the possibility that the type of politician attracted to legislative office may actually facilitate scandalous behavior—a facet of the problem of adverse selection.

Therefore, rent seeking contributes to the emergence of scandalous behavior in two ways. First, many scandals involve the outright exchange of political favors for money. Whether it is quashing government investigations as in the savings and loan debacle or accepting cash from Korean businessman Tongsun Park as in "Koreagate," the arrangement is the same: preferential treatment through the political process in return for income. The second way in which rent seeking fosters scandals has received far less attention: the manipulation of institutional arrangements by legislators with strong preferences for the financial rewards of legislative service. Simply put, rent-seeking individuals may use their positions to exploit institutional arrangements and the political process for financial gain; such activities erupt into public scandals once they are uncovered.

In the above paragraphs, I have only briefly touched upon some examples of the most obvious effect of rent seeking (exchange of political favors for money) in promoting congressional scandals. The second effect—the exploitation of institutional arrangements by rent seekers—is best illustrated by the involvement of rent-seeking legislators in the 1992 scandal at the House bank.

The House Bank Scandal

Some might say that Congress is "easy pickings" for individuals seeking to enhance their existing wealth. In fact, some institutional arrangements seem to facilitate wealth-earning activities such as rent seeking: the congressional patronage system (that primarily benefits the majority party) and the absence of internal mechanisms for *monitoring* and *policing* the activities of legislators are two arrangements that serve this objective. Majority party legislators exercise considerable leverage over patronage-appointed employees and such influence could be used to engage their assistance and cooperation in facilitating transactions that contribute to the personal wealth of legislators. The lack of mechanisms for monitoring and policing the actions of legislators assures some confidentiality to the dealings between the legislators interested in financial gain and the special interests who are willing to supply financial rewards in return for political favors.

Such arrangements are especially susceptible to exploitation if politicians within Congress covet financial rewards or are approaching their last term of office. Wealth-maximizing politicians seek out or create opportunities to exploit institutional arrangements for financial benefit: rent seeking could not prosper without their indulgence and cooperation. Legislators might be expected to refrain from such unethical behavior for fear of enraging voters and losing the next election. However, this electoral constraint will be insufficient to temper the rent-seeking behavior of politicians when they no longer face reelection—as in the last term of office before retirement. These conditions—a patronage-run organization, the absence of effective monitoring, the presence of a large number of rent seekers, and legislators facing retirement—were all present during the 1992 scandal at the House bank. Individually and collectively, these conditions shed light on why the bank scandal arose.

The scandal at the House bank involved check kiting. Check kiting is commonly defined as the writing of one check while knowing that there are insufficient funds in the account drawn upon and then attempting to cover the first check with a second check drawn on another account with insufficient funds. This situation aptly characterizes the behavior of some legislators toward the House bank. If legislators had the intent of running a check-kiting scheme, the operation of the House check-cashing facility offered a golden opportunity. The House bank had three specific advantages for wealth-maximizing individuals. First, legislators received an additional period of delay before they had to "make good" on a "bad" check. The practice was to accept rather than reject checks drawn by legislators despite insufficient funds; legislators would be contacted later and asked to make up the deficits. Second, legislators were aware that a bad check would never be sent back through channels without them first being informed and given a chance to cover the check. Finally, by honoring thousands of checks that most commercial banks would have returned (because of insufficient funds) the House bank permitted legislators to engage in conduct that would have been impossible, and possibly illegal, for the general public. Commercial bank check-kiting schemers could not have designed a more favorable set of conditions!

The House bank seems to epitomize the difficulty Congress has had in controlling opportunistic behavior. Until its demise in 1991, the House bank had operated for more than 150 years under informal rules and beyond any system of checks. At first glance, the House bank seems like a rather innocent endeavor: it was a depository where members could keep their salaries and money in checking accounts, and it was run by the office of the Sergeant at Arms and populated with patronage-appointed employees. Much like a commercial bank, the House bank took deposits, issued checkbooks, cashed checks, and issued monthly statements of deposits and debits. Unlike a commercial bank, however, the House bank did not pay interest on deposits, make interest-bearing loans, or invest bank assets for profit. The crucial distinction between commercial banks and the House bank, at least in terms of the focus of this analysis, is that the latter had a far more generous policy for handling bad checks than was the case at commercial banks.

Legislators who wrote checks for more money than they had in their accounts had little to worry about since the House bank would almost always honor them and delay collecting the debt until later. This is not how commercial banks handle overdrafts. Unless the individual who wrote the check has overdraft protection, commercial banks normally "bounce" such checks: the overdraft checks are returned to the person to whom they were written, and the check writer is charged a fee. If the account holder has overdraft protection, the bank issues a loan to cover the check and charges interest on the loan. Overdraft protection at a commercial bank is usually a line of credit, with a steep short-term interest rate. The total limit on overdraft protection depends on the credit worthiness of the account holder but rarely exceeds $5,000. The House bank reportedly had a higher limit (i.e., next month's net salary, about $7,000) and no interest or penalty.

The scandal was not that the House bank permitted check-bouncing; rather, the scandal involved the fact that the House bank refused to bounce checks. The bank rarely returned a legislator's bad check. Instead they paid the check and delayed charging the legislator until his or her account contained sufficient funds to cover the overdrafts. This procedure, in essence, rewarded legislators with interest-free loans: legislators did not merely bounce checks by issuing overdrafts; they "kited" checks. Bounced checks are returned to the payee because of insufficient funds in

the drawer's account; "kited" checks refer to bad checks or similar ficti-
tious or worthless financial instruments that are used to raise money or to
temporarily maintain credit.

The House bank's overdraft policy was never put in writing: legislators were only told about overdraft procedures if they inquired. No one
specifically informed members that they could write bad checks, but
neither did anyone insist that they could not. In fairness, it should be
noted that some House members were never actually notified that they
had overdrawn their accounts at the House bank, but these cases occurred primarily at the end of the month and were usually of small
consequence (i.e., the amount of the check would clearly be covered by
the next salary check due on the first day of the next month). The
habitual overdrafters, however, were persistently notified. In fact, one
employee of the bank devoted most of her time to making phone calls to
the delinquent members to notify them of their overdrafts.

Congressional records contain evidence of legislators making overdrafts at the House bank as far back as 1830. In modern times, the
General Accounting Office (GAO) did its first independent audit of the
House bank in 1947 and found overdrafts totaling $3,583. GAO audits
since then have regularly disclosed thousands of overdrafts that the bank
honored on a routine basis: 5,660 in 1963, 10,369 in 1969, and 12,309 in
1972. Clearly, the practice has grown. Moreover, the money involved in
these bank overdrafts is far from insignificant: for example, Carl Perkins
(D-Ky.) and Stephen Solarz (D-N.Y.) bounced over $500,000 worth of
checks in the 39-month GAO investigation (*Congressional Quarterly
Weekly Report*, April 4, 1992, 859).

Political and Economic Explanations for Check Kiting

Propositions drawn from both economics and political science provide
some clues as to why House members might get involved in kiting
checks. From the perspective of economic theory, the rational behavior
of legislators approaching retirement (the "last-period" problem) and
adverse selection in the type of politician coming to office offer valid
propositions for explaining check kiting at the House bank. Political
scientists might offer a different set of explanations, focusing on variables emphasizing the influence of power and the socialization of legislators to "institutional slack" (i.e., the lack of policing and monitoring in
Congress) in encouraging abuse of institutional prerogatives. These hypotheses are described in the following pages.

Last-period problems. Economists have become increasingly interested in the rational behavior of politicians when they no longer face an

electoral incentive (Lott 1987; Zupan 1990; Lott and Davis 1992). Rational politicians are expected to exploit their positions for gain when they no longer face the necessity of reelection—a process that keeps politicians faithful to their principals rather than their own principles. Therefore, rational politicians could be expected to "shirk" or neglect their responsibilities to their constituents and their duties in the legislature in the term prior to their retirement from the legislature. This is a problem that all institutions experience since retirement is always an option and could lead to just the type of pathologies associated with scandals in the House and Senate in recent years. Hence, we might attribute the parade of congressional scandals to politicians facing their last period of officeholding and rationally exploiting their positions for gain. Extending this logic to the scandal at the House bank, we might envision retiring legislators as taking advantage of the lax accounting procedures at the bank to obtain interest-free loans. Thus, one explanation for check kiting is that retiring legislators exploited their privileges at the House bank to a greater extent than did other legislators who faced reelection contests. The existence of a last-period problem would be indicated by a legislator announcing his or her retirement in 1991—prior to the public release of information about the abuses at the House bank. If there is a last-period problem inducing the abuse of office prerogatives, I expect retiring legislators to exploit their privileges at the House bank to a greater degree than other legislators who, in contrast, face a reelection campaign.

Adverse selection. As I noted in the introduction, economists have suggested that the body politic has been transformed into a rent-seeking society, with individuals and groups pursuing economic advantage vis-à-vis legislative acts and administrative regulations. These policies enable rent seekers to obtain valuable privileges, often earning monopoly-like profits and preventing competitors from contesting these returns. Politicians who are in a position to affect the rents obtained by groups and individuals stand to gain in a rent-seeking society; politicians eager to extract or expropriate some of the wealth or gain obtained through the policies they determine have good reason to gravitate toward those institutions that are susceptible, if not amenable, to rent-seeking behavior. Congress seems to be an especially attractive place to work for politicians seeking financial gain.

There are a number of characteristics that make Congress attractive to wealth-maximizing politicians. Only a few are briefly sketched here since these characteristics are elaborated upon in the next chapter. First, members of Congress exercise considerable influence over the distribution of rents, both because of the prominent role of Congress in enacting

legislation and the influence of individual members with federal agencies
(Fiorina 1977). Legislators, especially committee members, are in a position to shape public policy, thereby yielding leverage over rent-earning
legislation. And the intercession by congressmen in the affairs of federal
agencies often serves to influence the actions of these agencies (see, for
example, Faith, Leavens, and Tollison 1982). Such influence can be used
to assure that certain groups or individuals receive beneficial treatment in
the writing of federal regulations or are allowed exemptions from existing
regulations. Second, members have considerable freedom to exercise
discretion in Congress (Parker 1992a). Policy-making decentralization,
weak party leaders, and norms designed to protect the institutional independence of legislators (e.g., seniority, specialization) encourage and
support political independence. With such independence, legislators are
free to exploit the prerogatives of office without fear of punishment or
reprimand at the hands of their parties or leaders.

Finally, the lack of effective monitoring of the activities of legislators assures them a modicum of invisibility, enabling them to pursue
their own private interests without fear of being exposed by either party
leaders or voters. Indeed, the lack of monitoring seems to be an essential condition for the pursuit of personal gain (Alchian and Demsetz
1972). Freed from scrutiny, members of Congress face few constraints
on the pursuit of financial gain and self-interest: newspapers rarely follow individual members of Congress, and most information about the
behavior of members of Congress has its genesis in congressional or
district offices. Hence, information about members of Congress is both
sparse and biased in the member's favor.

Given these characteristics of Congress, there is ample reason for
those interested in financial gain to find legislative office attractive.
Rent-seeking politicians might be expected to abuse their privileges at
the House bank to a greater degree than other legislators because of
their interest in financial gain. Thus, the entrance of rent-seeking politicians into Congress—an evolutionary consequence of adverse selection—may explain abuses at the House bank. The indicator or measure
of a rent-seeking politician is the amount of honoraria collected in 1989
and 1990. Honoraria (e.g., payment for delivering a speech to a group)
function like rents: they are quasi-legal payments for services rendered
that normally exceed the opportunity cost of the service. I expect that
individuals who collected large honoraria, despite earning limits, have
stronger preferences for the wealth-generating aspects of the job than
others.

Socialization of freshmen. Some pathologies persist because a milieu exists that fosters the exploitation of legislative prerogatives. In

short, institutional abuse may be a learned or imitated response: only after years of congressional service do legislators learn how they can abuse their position with near *immunity*. This is not to argue that new entrants are too naive to exploit the prerogatives of office. Studies of congressional socialization have done considerable damage to the belief that new legislators lack sufficient sophistication and behave as neophytes in the legislative process. For one thing, legislators come to Congress aware of many informal norms (Asher 1973), and norms at odds with the goals of new legislators have gradually faded into obscurity (Rohde et al. 1985). Still, knowing basic legislative procedures, rules, and norms does not assure knowledge of how to exploit institutional prerogatives—these are lessons that come with experience and longevity in Congress.[2] Hence, we might expect freshmen members of Congress to be least disposed to exploiting the House bank system because they lack the information (or familiarity) on how to do so. Once they become socialized, however, freshmen become more aware of how they can exploit their positions for gain. Simply put, new legislators eventually learn of the permissive milieu that governs Congress and discourages harsh punishment of one's colleagues for wrongdoings (see chapter 7). Since the study of the House bank covers the period from 1988 to 1991, I consider freshmen members of Congress to be those taking office in 1987. Only these "new" legislators were present in Congress during the entire span of the study to qualify for inclusion in the analysis. In sum, freshmen members of Congress are expected to lack the information and experiences to exploit their privileges at the House bank to the same extent as their colleagues with longer tenure.

Political power. If there is one concept central to the study of politics, it is power. Power serves as a major explanation for why people contest for, and how they behave in, political office (Barber 1965; Fenno 1973) and delineates influential legislators from those less blessed as well. Positions of party leadership or committee and subcommittee chairmanships (or ranking minority member status) confer power on individual legislators, enabling them to exact a higher price for their cooperation than other legislators (Denzau and Munger 1986; Parker 1992b). Unfortunately, power may also exercise a corrupting influence on legislators. Journalistic references to the "arrogance of power" and adages

---

2. Tenure might seem a better measure of institutional socialization: the longer one's career in Congress, the more information obtained about the functioning of the institution. Tenure, however, is strongly correlated with membership in the party leadership corps, robbing both variables of statistical significance when they are introduced into the same equation. The equation including tenure, but excluding the dummy variables for freshmen representatives and party leadership, is not statistically significant.

such as "power corrupts," are constant reminders that power has an adverse impact on its wielder.

Power might be viewed as corrupting even well-intentioned individuals into believing that they are above the rules and laws that operate on the citizenry and govern political institutions. Hence, they exploit their positions of power and the prerogatives of office. Since the congressional patronage system is one of the significant prerogatives of power—normally a reward of majority party status—we might expect legislators in positions of power to abuse patronage arrangements to a greater degree than those lacking such power. In short, I expect powerful legislators to kite more checks than others. I examine two measures of political power: position as a party or committee leader and membership in the majority party. Both of these characteristics are important sources of institutional influence and can be expected to carry considerable weight with patronage-run organizations like the House bank.

Statistical model and analysis. The functional relationships between the number of check overdrafts between July 1, 1988, and October 3, 1991, and the above variables can be specified in the following manner:

$$C = f(M, H, F, R, P), \tag{1}$$

where

C = number of check overdrafts,
M = whether or not legislator is a member of the minority party (Republicans); coded as 2.7183 if legislator is a Republican and 1 if legislator is a Democrat,
H = the total amount of honoraria raised by the legislator in 1989 and 1990,
F = whether or not legislator was a freshman representative in 1986; coded as 2.7183 if legislator was a freshman in 1986 and 1 if he or she was *not* a new entrant,
R = whether or not legislator announced his or her retirement prior to 1992; coded as 2.7183 if legislator announced his or her retirement and 1 if he or she planned to seek reelection, and
P = whether or not legislator holds a position of party leadership (i.e., party, committee leader or ranking minority member); coded 2.7183 if the legislator is a member of the party's top leadership corps and 1 if he or she is not an occupant of a top leadership position.

The analysis is based on all representatives who were present for the entire period during which House bank records were examined (July 1, 1988, to October 3, 1991).

Since most members, if queried, would probably echo the electorally correct response—namely, opposition to the House bank and its loose procedures—we cannot really know their true preferences for latitude at the House bank. One mechanism that forces individuals to reveal their preferences is "voting." Voting can assume a variety of forms (see, for instance, Tiebout 1956), and writing a check overdraft can be viewed as a mechanism of voting (or revealing) one's preferences. Thus, I view "check-bouncing" as a preference-revealing mechanism through which legislators, by taking advantage of the loose House banking procedures, register their preferences for these privileges. Hence, the more checks bounced, the stronger a member's preference ("demand") for latitude at the House bank. Like most consumption activities studied by economists, I assume bank abuse to yield diminishing marginal benefit or utility for House members. That is, legislators who bounce a considerable number of checks eventually experience diminishing marginal utility with successive overdrafts. Thus, legislators are assumed to be utility-maximizers who express their preference for the latitude provided at the House bank by writing check overdrafts thereby exploiting their privileges at the bank. However, diminished marginal utility accompanies the continued exploitation of privileges at the House bank (i.e., the utility obtained through check-bouncing increases at a decreasing rate). This assumption is not essential to the analysis but maintains important continuity between economic theory and the study of rent-seeking behavior in Congress.[3]

The results of the analysis are shown in table 1. It is clear from this table that retiring legislators display no greater tendency toward exploiting their prerogatives at the House bank in their last term (period) of officeholding than continuing members. We cannot, however, discount

---

3. These assumptions necessitate a logarithmic transformation of the variables in the analysis to assure that the functional form of the theoretical model is consistent with the assumptions guiding the analysis. A logarithmic transformation also reduces the influence of outliers found in the data and improves upon the statistical fit of the model to the data. Since I am using several dummy variables in my analysis (i.e., M, F, R, P), and I have assumed a logarithmic function to the writing of check overdrafts, it is necessary to transform all of the variables in the analysis to their logarithmic equivalents. This explains why the dummy variables are coded as 2.7183 and 1 rather than 1 and zero (0): zero is undefined as a logarithm. To prevent this problem from confounding my analysis, I have translated 1 and 0 into their natural logarithmic equivalents—2.7183 and 1; the natural logs of these latter two numbers are 1 and 0 respectively.

TABLE 1. Predictors of Check Kiting at the House Bank

Variables	b	t-value	Significance	Tobit Estimate	t-value
Minority party member (M)	−.730	−3.392	.001	−1.100	−3.418
Honoraria income (H)	.081	3.302	.001	.112	3.046
Freshman legislator (F)	−.645	−2.103	.036	−.967	−2.084
Retiring member of Congress (R)	.111	.183	.855	.273	.312
Party leader (P)	.168	.587	.558	.040	.095
Constant	1.603	6.053	.000	.901	2.277
Statistics:					
Multiple R		.28			
F-statistic		5.91			
Significance		.000			
N		352			
Log likelihood		−729.26		−660.72	

the importance of the socialization that takes place in Congress, alerting some neophytes to the extralegislative benefits of officeholding: freshmen legislators kited far fewer checks than their more senior colleagues. Adverse selection may also be at work here, creating a milieu that is supportive of (or neutral to) institutional abuses, thereby encouraging new legislators to "join in."

Two additional factors exercised a more pronounced influence (alpha < .001) on check kiting: power and the existence of a large number of rent seekers. Membership in the minority party reduced the number of checks bounced; *majority* party members exploited their privileges at the House bank to a greater degree than their minority party colleagues. Top party leaders, however, did not abuse their prerogatives at the House bank to a greater degree than other party members. A particularly important factor related to abuse at the House bank was the behavior of rent seekers. Not surprisingly, the same features that make Congress such an integral part of the rent-seeking society also make it an attractive place for rent seekers to practice their trade. Such legislators seem to have been a major source of abuse at the House bank.[4]

---

4. Since there are many observations (legislators) with values of zero on the dependent variable (i.e., they have not kited any checks at the House bank), tobit may be a more appropriate estimation technique; as is clear from table 1, irrespective of the statistical technique, the findings remain the same. There has been some empirical research suggesting that the political philosophy of legislators affects their discretionary behavior. For instance, James Bennett and Thomas DiLorenzo (1982) found that conservative senators returned a larger percentage of their (unspent) staff budgets to the U.S. Treasury than did their liberal colleagues. In order to explore the possibility that political ideology con-

The findings can now be summarized. There is little empirical support for the notion that Congress faces serious problems when members decide to retire: retiring legislators showed no greater inclination to abuse their check-writing privileges at the House bank than continuing members. If there is a last-period problem, I found no evidence of its pathological effect (I examine this important proposition again in chapter 6). There is evidence, however, that legislators in positions of political (but not institutionalized) power and those with large honoraria incomes abused their privileges at the House bank to a greater degree than other members. Majority party members (Democrats) kited more checks than Republicans and the higher a legislator's honoraria earnings were, the more he or she kited.

Summary

A major premise of this book is that not all of the gain obtained through political office is financial. There are many intrinsic benefits to public service that are often ignored in strictly economic treatments of the motives of officeholders. Richard Fenno (1973) suggests that legislators are motivated by the desire to create "good public policy," and Joseph Kalt and Mark Zupan (1990) demonstrate that legislators make altruistic decisions. There are still other intrinsic benefits associated with public service: some politicians increase their utility by helping others or serving their version of the public good; other politicians believe public service is an obligation that validates their image as an ideal citizen; and still others experience a feeling of contentment derived not so much from helping others as from their membership in a prestigious political institution. Aside from the desire to serve the public interest, other factors generating utility for politicians include the prestige associated with public office, pride, institutional influence, friendships, and commitments to specific causes.

If the intrinsic benefits from government service persist, we can expect institutions to attract recruits who value these returns highly. On the other hand, if intrinsic benefits cannot be obtained in sufficient quantity through legislative service, individuals preferring such rewards to monetary gain will pursue other avenues of public service. A decline (or loss) in the intrinsic benefits associated with congressional service

---

strained abuses at the House bank, I introduced a measure of legislator personal ideology—ratings of House members by the liberal Americans for Democratic Action (ADA)—into the model equation predicting the number of check overdrafts. This variable is excluded from the final model reported here because *none* of the coefficients associated with ADA ratings ever attained statistical significance.

may even make the material benefits of congressional service far more relevant in enticing individuals to office. If so, Congress could eventually become dominated by those who value more the material benefits from legislative service. In a rent-seeking society, it is easy to understand why service in the legislature might be highly valued by politicians more interested in wealth than public service.

There are several implications that can be drawn from the analysis of the 1992 House bank scandal. First, scandals may be more than idiosyncratic, remote events; they may be symptoms of emerging institutional problems. Second, the age-old adages about the correlation between power and abuse seem to account for some of the liberties that members took at the House bank. For example, legislators in the majority party appear to have exploited their prerogatives to a greater degree than others. Third, we should be deeply concerned that the power of Congress to influence the economic well-being of individual citizens may result in some form of adverse selection where politicians interested in financial gain seek legislative office and exploit congressional procedures and arrangements.

Institutions may evolve in ways that make them attractive to certain types of individuals within society; such individuals may even contribute to the evolution of an institution by modifying institutional arrangements to facilitate the realization of private, personal goals (Fiorina 1977; Parker 1986; Parker 1992a). Even those who come to politics with loftier motives may succumb if the general institutional milieu is supportive of, or indifferent to, rent-seeking behavior. Armen Alchian (1950) has argued that institutions evolve so that only the fittest survive—those who earn "positive profits." Politicians interested in increasing their own wealth can look to Congress for the opportunity to do so; they can earn considerable "profits" from public service. If psychic and nonmaterial rewards for government service fade (e.g., the public esteem of legislators, gratitude for governmental service), those who remain in office may be primarily preoccupied with financial gain.

This chapter has been devoted to exploring the adverse selection hypothesis that rent seekers manipulate and abuse institutional arrangements for financial gain. The behavior of rent seekers in abusing their privileges at the House bank suggests that one way of controlling rent seeking in Congress is by increasing the attractiveness of legislative service for those with distinct preferences for the intrinsic rewards of a congressional career. But has the evolution of Congress resulted in this type of member coming to Congress? This question serves as the focus for the next chapter.

CHAPTER 4

Adverse Selection and the Composition of Congress

Nobel economist James Buchanan (1980, 13–14) has identified three "levels" or expressions of rent seeking. First, if the rights to recover rents are neither distributed equally, randomly, nor through an auction process, then prospective entrants will engage in rent seeking through efforts to persuade officials to grant them differentially advantageous treatment. This form of rent seeking is commonly associated with legislative lobbying. Second, if the salaries and perquisites of governmental employment contain elements of economic rents and are higher than those in comparable vocations, prospective politicians and bureaucrats will "waste" major resources attempting to secure the favored posts. Excessive spending on campaigns for congressional office, for example, could be driven by the attractiveness of the rents open to capture through governmental office. Finally, the attempts of groups and individuals to secure differentially favorable treatment or to avoid adverse economic treatment through the governmental fiscal process are also expressions of rent seeking. The efforts of groups to secure favorable tax treatment or to avoid unfavorable treatment, are common examples of this third form of rent seeking. To this list we can add a fourth expression of rent seeking: adverse selection.[1]

---

1. Three of the forms of rent-seeking behavior mentioned above have received considerable empirical investigation and support. For example, lobbying Congress has become such an established feature of the legislative landscape that members of Congress accord considerable legitimacy to the role of groups in the political process (Aberbach and Rockman 1978). We can also find evidence of excesses in campaign spending; high levels of campaign expenditures have become the expectation rather than the exception. Incumbents need not worry about emptying their campaign coffers since they normally can raise as much campaign money as they need or want (Goldenberg and Traugott 1984). Finally, numerous case studies of regulations or specific laws demonstrate that the political process can be exploited to promote wealth transfers or rents. The influence of railroad interests on Interstate Commerce Commission policies is one well-documented example (see, for instance, Gilligan, Marshall, and Weingast 1989 for an analysis of the formation of the Interstate Commerce Act of 1887). In contrast to the attention given these three forms of rent seeking, little effort has been devoted to the question of adverse selection.

The notion of "adverse selection" is derived, in part, from Armen Alchian's contention that the economic system evolves so that only those who earn positive profits (returns) from their participation in that system will be "selected" as survivors. In Alchian's words, "those who realize *positive profits* are the survivors; those who suffer losses disappear" (1950, 213). Alchian's argument directs our attention to the returns available through legislative service since only those legislators who can obtain positive (i.e., satisfactory) returns from such service remain members. If the chief returns from a congressional career somehow shift from intrinsic (the rewards of officeholding itself) to material (rents), those obtaining positive "profits" from their service in the institution may also change: the institution becomes more attractive to those with preferences for financial gain and less attractive to those who prefer intrinsic rewards to financial ones. In addition, if there are significant economic benefits to officeholding arising from the opportunities available for appropriating or extracting rents from others doing business with government, then people may be attracted to public office for the wrong reasons. This is particularly critical if the intrinsic benefits of officeholding diminish to the point that those seeking such intrinsic gains pursue different careers. Hence, the institution may eventually become populated by some of the least public-serving individuals.

My argument also builds upon George Akerlof's (1970) clever insight about why the used car market eventually disintegrates into a market for worthless automobiles—cars with mechanical problems, widely referred to as "lemons." Akerlof argues that people trade in "lemons" because good used cars and bad ones sell at the same price. Hence, people with good cars won't trade them in on new ones for fear of obtaining a lemon and because they won't receive the car's true worth. The result is a market where only lemons are available: "most cars traded will be the 'lemons,' and good cars may not be traded at all" (1970, 489). The same dynamics may operate in the market for congressional recruits: through adverse selection, the only politicians interested in holding office in an institution with few intrinsic returns may also be "lemons"!

If individuals are attracted to legislative service for the wrong reason—for example, wealth maximization—we can expect the price of governance to increase since rent-seeking legislators drive up the costs of doing business with the government and ultimately the costs to society. Such conditions constitute a form of adverse selection: Congress may evolve to the point that those seeking intrinsic rewards are unable to obtain a satisfactory return from service in the legislature and either depart or eschew congressional office. "The cost of dishonesty," Akerlof observed, "lies not only in the amount by which the purchaser is cheated; the cost also must include the loss incurred from driving legitimate business out of existence" (1970, 495).

Some Institutional Effects of Adverse Selection

If adverse selection is allowed to shape the evolution of Congress, several negative consequences might be expected. One of the major propositions of rational choice models of legislatures is that legislators manipulate institutional arrangements to further their own selfish objectives. For instance, Morris Fiorina (1977) and David Mayhew (1974) contend that institutional arrangements are molded to promote electoral safety. If members of Congress modify institutional arrangements to promote reelection, we might expect them to do the same when the quest is for rents rather than electoral safety. The exploitation of check-cashing privileges at the House bank by legislators receiving large honoraria income, discussed in chapter 3, is one clear example of rent seekers manipulating institutional arrangements. Thus, as a result of adverse selection, a critical or sufficient mass of rent-seeking politicians might contrive to change institutional rules and structures to enhance wealth-earning opportunities, manipulating institutional arrangements in a perverse manner.

As new generations of legislators come to Washington, seeking to enhance their existing wealth by engaging in rent seeking and altering institutional arrangements to facilitate their rent-seeking activities, eventually the institution will become more accommodative to the rent-seeking demands of its members. As a consequence, acknowledged legislative skills (e.g., prior legislative office) lose significance for service in Congress. Talents for bargaining, debating, drafting legislation, and coalition-building lose relevance in a rent-seeking legislature as other skills gain prominence—such as raising campaign funds, stimulating demand for rent-seeking services by clientele interests, escaping monitoring. In short, skills relevant to extracting large rents from groups seeking legislative action (or bureaucratic help, for that matter) will eventually overshadow those essential for legislating in a rent-seeking society.

Finally, adverse selection is likely to impact negatively on the evolution of an institution in another significant way: the exit of career politicians. As noted in chapter 2, legislators preferring the intrinsic rewards of congressional service see a legislative career as a valuable good or commodity, while those preferring financial returns to intrinsic ones see congressional service as largely a vehicle for profit. Given the spirit of mutual noninterference that marks collegial relations in Congress, we might expect legislators preferring intrinsic returns to financial rewards to care little how those preferring material returns behave. Perhaps, but if we assume that rent seeking within the legislature reduces the intrinsic returns of a congressional career, then legislators preferring intrinsic returns have reason to exit because the returns from officeholding will decline to the point that the costs of service are greater than the intrinsic returns. If the intrinsic rewards of a congressional career rise with longevity in office, legislators establishing long careers obtain the greatest intrinsic returns. They also suffer most when rent-seeking actions reduce these returns. Therefore, the adverse selection of rent seekers eventually increases the exit of legislators who have established long congressional careers. These negative externalities of the rent-seeking society (and adverse selection) cannot be easily ignored. Such behavior creates "deadweight losses" in the production of legislation by introducing inefficiencies into the process, diverting resources, and promoting conditions conducive to pathological behavior (e.g., bribery, selling of votes, extorting favors from groups doing business with government).

Adverse selection has the potential to become a major problem in the evolution of Congress because the institution has been held in low regard for long periods of time and possesses characteristics that make it an unusually inviting target for those seeking financial gain. Low public regard reduces the stature of Congress and therefore the intrinsic returns that can be derived from legislative service. Institutional features provide numerous opportunities to extract rents from groups doing business with government while shielding these activities from scrutiny and reprimand.

Public Esteem of Politicians and Institutions

As long as congressional service is highly valued by society, talented and experienced politicians will seek office. When the job of the member of Congress, and the institution in which he or she serves, are viewed with public contempt, respected politicians will steer clear of the opportunity to serve. This is exactly the situation evolving in Congress: the intrinsic benefits are gradually disappearing as the public's negative view of members of Congress and Congress itself demeans and denigrates legislative service. If left unabated, the major benefit of a congressional career ultimately may become the financial gain obtained by serving as an intermediary in dealings between rent-seeking groups and government. Under such conditions, politicians attracted to legislative service may place a higher premium on the rent-seeking possibilities of congressional office than on the intrinsic benefits associated with service in an unpopular political institution.

Legislators are quite cognizant of, and sensitive to, public contempt and disrespect. "A vast gulf remains between the perceptions many Americans have of Congress (privileged, untrustworthy, inefficient) and the view most lawmakers have of themselves" (Merida 1994, 13). The remarks of two retiring legislators probably echo the feelings of a lot of senior members:

> People just presume we are dishonorable. I don't know if you have ever been suspected of doing something dishonest, but if you have you know it is not a pleasant feeling until you are cleared. Well, imagine living under a cloud of suspicion all the time. If you can do that, you can understand why some of us think serving in Congress isn't enjoyable.

> The vilification of the average politician in the eyes of the public is a very alarming trend. It makes it less pleasant for us to go out in public. We all like to be proud of the work we do, but some people seem to think I should be ashamed to have served in the U.S. Congress. (Hibbing 1982a, 63; see also, Craig 1993, 146–48)

These perceptions probably deter some of the most capable and experienced politicians from seeking congressional office. Thus, a manifestation of adverse selection may occur: public-spirited citizens avoid congressional service because they cannot expect to derive sufficient intrinsic benefits from legislative service, relative to the costs involved in obtaining and sustaining a legislative career. There is ample evidence from public opinion surveys that neither the job of the legislator nor the institutional performance of Congress receive high praise from citizens.

Public opinion. Most political offices yield intrinsic returns to those interested in public service per se. These returns are in the form of such things as the positive feeling of contributing to the welfare of society, its governance, and the solution of societal problems. These may not seem very valuable benefits, especially given the costs—opportunity and otherwise—required in obtaining political office. But for elites who have accomplished many kinds of economic, academic, and social goals, political office may be a rational pursuit—the value being the inherent nature of public service. Thus, these individuals invest their scarcest and most dear resource—themselves—in political careers, making many personal, economic, and professional sacrifices along the way.

These investments are expected to yield intrinsic returns over the length of their careers in office. As long as the intrinsic benefits are greater than the costs involved in officeholding, public-spirited individuals will invest in political careers. The intrinsic benefits associated with political office are at least partially a function of how the office is publicly evaluated. Simply put, esteemed professions yield greater intrinsic returns than vocations held in lower regard. If political office is demeaned or denigrated, the intrinsic benefits associated with that office will eventually diminish. Hence, the costs of public service may outweigh the intrinsic benefits thereby reducing the incentives to hold office among those most dedicated and committed to doing so.

With respect to the U.S. Congress, we might expect dedicated public servants who value the intrinsic returns from officeholding to steer away from legislative service for several reasons. First, respected politicians may shy away from congressional service because the ethical standards are perceived as quite low, reducing the esteem associated with congressional office. Second, individuals seeking intrinsic benefits may avoid legislative service because Congress is viewed as a poor investment of one's time and effort. If intrinsic benefits are not forthcoming because of the low esteem of congressional service, dedicated public servants will not rationally invest in a congressional career because of the poor return on that investment. Third, honorable politicians may steer clear of congressional service because of the fear that their own reputations will be tarnished thereby destroying the reputational capital they have already accumulated.[2]

While politics has never been held in very high regard as a vocation, the esteem of politicians appears to have undergone further erosion in recent decades. For instance, politicians and legislators are increasingly viewed as ignoring voters while paying attention to "big interests" (fig. 3). In 1964, 29 percent of those surveyed in a national opinion survey believed that a "few big interests ran government," but in 1984, the percentage rose to 55 percent. Similarly, in 1968, 32 percent of those surveyed believed that most members of Congress paid "a good deal" of attention to the people who elect them when they decide what to do in Congress, but by 1980, only 17 percent perceived the same level of responsiveness (fig. 4). Ten years later, in 1990, only 12 percent perceived a "great deal" of responsiveness (*American Enterprise* 1992, 83). The same pattern is observed when voters are queried about how much

---

2. It might be argued that low levels of institutional esteem mean little to legislators since they are normally well loved by their constituents and that is what really counts. However, institutional esteem is related to voter perceptions of their own member of Congress. For example, lack of confidence in Congress diminishes an individual's trust in their own representative (Parker and Parker 1993). In sum, declining institutional esteem does have an impact—and a decidedly negative effect—on certain components of the image of individual members of Congress among their constituents.

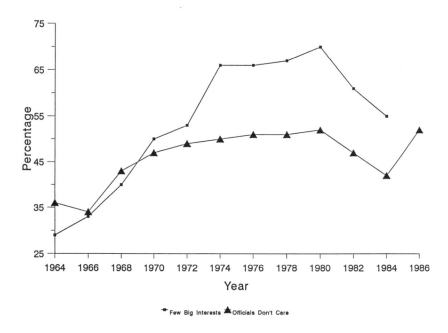

Fig. 3. Who runs the government? (Data from National Election Studies 1964–86.)

public officials care about constituents: 36 percent of those surveyed in 1964 agreed that public officials don't "care much what people like me think," but by 1986, the proportion had risen to 52 percent (fig. 3); 53 percent of those surveyed in 1968 agreed with the statement that "those we elect to Congress in Washington lose touch with the people pretty quickly," but by 1980, 71 percent agreed with this statement (fig. 4). Throughout the 1980s, more than three of five voters believed that "most members of Congress care more about keeping power than they do about the best interests of the nation" (*American Enterprise* 1992, 83); in 1994, 83 percent of those interviewed agreed with this statement (*ABC News/Washington Post Poll,* June 23–26, 1994).

Whatever trend may underlie these data the common theme is a greater public suspicion of the motives of politicians in general and members of Congress in particular. For example, about 45 percent of those interviewed in 1976 believed that most members of Congress act more in their own self-interest than the best interests of the public (table 2), but by 1990, 58 percent believed legislators were more interested in benefiting themselves (*American Enterprise* 1992, 83). Most Americans

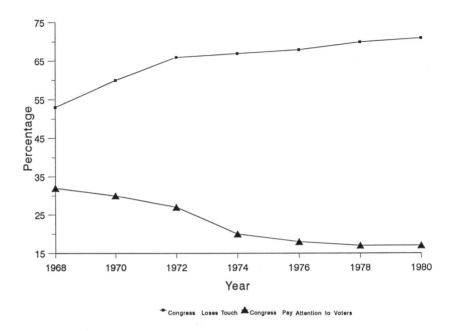

Fig. 4. Does Congress serve the people? (Data from National Election Studies 1968–80.)

TABLE 2.   What Motivates Legislators?

Question: "Do you think most (Congressmen, Senators) tend to act more in their own self-interest, or more in the public interest?"

Motivation	Members of Congress (%)	Senators (%)
Self-interest	46.6	45.1
Public interest	41.2	41.8
Don't know	12.1	13.1
N	1998	1998

Source: Data from Roper Surveys, Study #76-8, August 1976.

do not feel that members of Congress "have a high personal moral code" (60 percent) or "care deeply about the problems of ordinary citizens" (69 percent) (*ABC News/Washington Post Poll,* June 23–26, 1994). Such suspicion reduces the esteem of politicians and legislators thereby diminishing the intrinsic returns to officeholding.

In addition to growing public skepticism regarding the extent to which politicians are sensitive to the opinions of voters, some notable recruits are probably deterred from seeking congressional office because of the perception that the institution is populated by unsavory characters. Opinion surveys focusing on the ethics of various professions consistently demonstrate the low esteem in which politicians, especially legislators, are held. Seymour Lipset and William Schneider, for example, concluded after an extensive analysis of opinion polls that "ethical standards are considered high in the 'service' professions (education, science, medicine, religion, the military) and low in most areas of the economy and government, including business, labor, politics, and the bureaucracy" (1983, 79–80). They suggested that "the principal difference between the positively regarded professions and the negatively evaluated ones would appear to be the varying importance of self-interest." Simply put, many citizens apparently believe that those who go into public life do so in order to advance their own private interests (table 2). The picture of Congress that is suggested by these public images seems certain to diminish the intrinsic returns of a legislative career. Who thirsts to serve in an institution where legislators are perceived as making "a lot of money by using public office improperly" (57 percent); "telling lies if they feel the truth will hurt them politically" (76 percent); and serving in a corrupt institution (50 percent) (*American Enterprise* 1992, 84)?

Table 3 presents the results of a survey of American public opinion toward the ethics of people running various public and private institutions. Congress fares poorly in most comparisons: only the ethics of those running labor unions and major corporations are perceived to be

TABLE 3.　Institutional Ethics

Question: "Now, I'd like to ask how you would describe the ethics of people running various institutions—very high, somewhat high, somewhat low, or very low?"

	Very High (%)	Somewhat High (%)	Somewhat Low (%)	Very Low (%)	N.S. (%)
Major corporations	9	36	29	14	12
White House	17	43	24	8	8
Organized labor	8	26	32	22	13
Television news	20	46	21	7	6
Newspapers	16	47	24	7	7
Congress	10	44	29	9	9
State governors and their administrations	12	47	23	7	11

Source: Data from U.S. House Commission on Administrative Review 1977.

lower than those who serve in Congress. It is not clear how or why these images of Congress, and those who serve within, are so cynical. Some of the cynicism may be due to the actions of legislators themselves who often denigrate the institution when in their constituencies (Fenno 1978) as well as the onslaught of congressional scandals in recent decades. Whatever the source, such cynicism diminishes the intrinsic returns to congressional office, and, unfortunately, public disapprobation appears to be on the rise.

Institutional Characteristics Facilitating Rent Seeking

It is not merely the low esteem of Congress that makes the institution so susceptible to adverse selection. The nature of political institutions may also entice recruits who lack a dedication to public service but see institutions as possessing attributes conducive to the promotion of private (rather than public) interests. The words of then British Governor General of India Warren Hastings in defending himself against charges of malfeasance in the nineteenth century—"when I consider my opportunities," he told the House of Lords, "I can but marvel at my moderation"—may seem humorous but they call attention to the numerous opportunities afforded politicians to exploit institutional arrangements for financial gain. What are the characteristics, then, that make Congress an unusually attractive place for politicians seeking to gain from the rent-seeking society? Probably the primary characteristic that would attract wealth-maximizers to congressional service is the capacity of Congress to influence rent-earning legislation and regulations. Congress's role in the policy process assures that legislators will have considerable say in who benefits from governmental decisions. This role encourages groups to focus their efforts on the legislature. Hence, there is a ready-made market for the services of legislators, and they need never worry about finding buyers or generating business.

Not only do legislatures pass laws that yield rents, they also exercise influence within the federal bureaucracy that enables them to help their "friends" obtain regulations or special treatment, such as exemptions to regulations. The federal bureaucracy can be viewed as serving the purposes of rent-seeking legislators in still another more devious way: the bureaucracy facilitates the ability of legislators to maximize the compensation they receive for their services! A major problem confronting rational politicians in extracting compensation is how much to demand. Members of Congress expecting to receive a "pay-off" (for example, campaign contributions) for helping a group or industry obtain rent-earning legislation must have some idea of the size of the wealth transfers they are effecting. This requires specialized knowledge, and legislators cannot expect their clients—groups and industries—to supply such information (i.e., they have no incentive to reveal this information, and even if they did, would legislators believe the estimates?). The federal bureaucracy has the capacity to supply such information because of the extensive data in the possession of individual agencies, and the technical expertise supplied by these agencies to legislators (GAO, for example). Once legislators know the economic effects of the legislation they enact, they can "charge" accordingly; bureaucratic agencies earn the favor and support of legislators by supplying these economic estimates, and rent-extracting legislators are able to obtain the largest monetary returns possible.

Institutional characteristics function in two additional ways to make Congress attractive to rent-seeking politicians. First, the decentralized nature of Congress enhances the ability of *individual* legislators to influence the content of regulations and laws. Second, existing institutional controls on the avarice and discretion of legislators are exceedingly weak. These characteristics make rent seeking an attractive feature of congressional service. In the following pages, I discuss how institutional arrangements might create fertile conditions for the adverse selection of rent-extracting politicians to congressional service.

Ability to influence public policy. While individual members are rarely prominent or decisive in the formation of major national policies, each member has considerable influence over a more narrow set of public policies—regulations—that may be even more profitable for groups than the actual legislation that gave birth to the regulations (Stigler 1971). The influence of individual members is derived from three facts of legislative life: the congressional process is decentralized; legislators have personal and political influence over federal agencies through their committee assignments—the "cozy triangle" phenomenon; and legislators exercise considerable independence.

The decentralization of congressional power is reflected in the autonomy of subunits, like committees and subcommittees in Congress, and the capacity of committee members to serve as sources of information and advice. As policy experts, committee members often gain the support of "indifferent" legislators who have little knowledge or interest in the policies a committee member may be espousing. By enlisting the support of the indifferent, individual members can multiply their influence over policies they strongly favor. Even the power of congressional committees is subject to decentralization: power within committees is spread among committee factions and subcommittees. Policies are formulated within small bodies—subcommittees—that enhance the power of individual members, and voting blocs within committees coalesce among like-minded members to dominate most policy outcomes (Parker and Parker 1985). This decentralization ensures that individual members will have a modicum of power to affect policies important to groups. Moreover, the decentralized nature of the congressional process ensures that *many* legislators stand to gain: since the legislative process is a morass of hurdles, the acquiescence of many legislators (e.g., logrolling) is frequently required to pass rent-earning legislation. Hence, those who seek to appropriate some of the wealth being transferred to groups or industries have ample opportunities to do so.

Congressional committees also serve as important conduits for member influence over federal regulations and service to organized groups. The term cozy triangle captures the essence of the relationship between federal agencies, congressional committees and subcommittees, and organized groups (Parker 1989). Among the factors that bring these participants together in the political process is a common goal: each has a vital interest in the maintenance and growth of regulations. For example, regulations earn agencies greater programmatic responsibility and accompanying budget increases; regulations also help groups and industries increase their profits by restricting competition and legislators gain because they are rewarded with campaign funds and electoral support (Stigler 1971). Finally, legislators help groups by influencing agency decisions regarding the establishment or interpretation of regulations. Such symbiotic arrangements benefit all parties, and therefore few seek to seriously reform this subgovernment phenomenon (see, for example, Davidson and Oleszek 1977).

Committees are critical elements in the system that delivers benefits to groups and industries for at least two reasons. First, a committee not only exercises control over an agency's budget, but it also has a virtual monopoly over all policies and programs related to an agency. This enhances a committee's ability to veto any legislation relating to an agency that is introduced by committee outsiders. In essence, the committee system represents an implicit trade: legislators trade their control over a large number of decisions for exclusive control over a smaller set of policies that matter more to them. Second, committees are populated largely through a process of self-selection: although there are differing estimates of the rate of success in obtaining preferred assignments (Gertzog 1976; Cox and McCubbins 1993, 40–42), most legislators obtain their preferred assignment rather quickly. Hence, there are few ponderous obstacles to the self-selection process. This means that members of Congress with interest in extracting a fee for serving rent-seeking groups can gravitate to those committees that do the most business in this regard. The result is an overrepresentation that makes it easier to serve group interests.

A major characteristic of members of Congress is that they exercise considerable latitude in the pursuit of their personal interests in Washington. Even institutional norms that once constrained expressions of independence, like the apprenticeship norm, appear to be on the wane. Congress has historically been quite tolerant of individualistic behavior, even rather offensive displays of independence (Huitt 1961). This independence of members of Congress permeates their policy-making behavior: legislators operate as individual policy entrepreneurs promoting policies and regulations, often on a unilateral basis. While such behavior may not be conducive to the interests of centralized political authorities, congressional party leaders tolerate legislator independence nonetheless.

The entrepreneurial activities of legislators serve a number of objectives. For example, entrepreneurial legislators advance causes that might not serve the parochial interests of voters. Unfortunately, they can also use their skills in the legislative process to help groups obtain rent-earning legislation. Enterprising legislators always can find creative ways to serve groups (e.g., exploiting personal friendships within agencies) and to extract rents for themselves in the process (e.g., threatening groups with taxes). Even repealing regulations under the guise of cutting red tape, might be worth something to groups. Since all members gain from the freedom to pursue their own private interests, efforts to constrain such latitude often encounter severe opposition. In the absence of public outrage, there are few incentives for individual legislators to support and promote restrictions on their own freedom. Under this guise of legislator independence, the range of acceptable behavior is quite wide. This enables wealth-maximizing legislators to extract rents from groups without having to worry about interference from others inside Congress. Perhaps Congress is too tolerant of individualistic behavior or fails to adequately discriminate between expressions of legislator independence and violations of reasonable codes of conduct? In any event, few have cause to question the entrepreneurial efforts of legislators motivated by rent extractions; to do so threatens the freedom that all legislators enjoy and forces value judgments that members of Congress seem reticent to make.

Weak controls over legislators. Another reason why individuals attracted to the rent-earning capacity of the legislature might seek congressional office is that there are only modest or weak controls over the behavior of legislators. We might expect the necessity of reelection, the existence of centralized party leaders, the public nature of the legislative process, and the force of internal congressional norms to be sufficient to control or restrain the avarice of legislators, and these influences probably do so to some degree. However, these mechanisms are too frequently ineffective. Weakened political parties and leaders, substantial incumbent electoral safety, lack of monitoring, and the persistence of norms promoting "mutual noninterference" all operate to reduce the effectiveness of existing controls on the behavior of today's legislators.

For one thing, Congress is characterized by a lack of party discipline. Rather than disciplined parties, like those in many parliamentary systems, congressional parties represent coalitions of factions and subgroups that normally exhibit only a minimum amount of loyalty to their leaders. Party leaders are more likely to bargain with their followers than to cajole them, and few believe that threatening members with the loss of some valued project or position does any good in promoting leadership support. One reason party leaders appear to exercise less influence on their members today than in the past is because they lack the resources to influence goal attainment and are apprehensive about punishing members in any way. Hence, leadership threats are relatively hollow, and leaders and party members recognize that fact. Party leaders are even unlikely to withhold rewards from those who oppose them!

Thus, rent-extracting politicians need not worry about central leaders reprimanding or punishing them for the pursuit of financial gain. Of course, wealth-maximizing legislators do not operate with the blessings of their party leaders. Nonetheless, there is little that party leaders can do to prevent rent seeking or to discourage wealth-maximizing politicians from practicing their trade in the legislative arena. One reason why leaders exercise little influence over party members is because legislators are not dependent upon their parties for their electoral survival and success; without an electoral incentive, legislators have little need to follow the directives of party leaders.

Elections might seem an appropriate mechanism for controlling the wealth-maximizing tendencies of legislators, but the electoral safety of House incumbents suggests that few legislators need worry about electoral reprisals. Figure 5 describes the trend in the electoral safety of House incumbents: the percentage of incumbents winning by at least 60 percent of the vote has been rising. In recent years more than 70 percent of the incumbents running for reelection are returned to office by safe election margins. This is not to argue that transgressions, once uncovered, never hasten electoral defeat. On the contrary, there are a sufficient number of instances where ethically dishonest legislators were removed by the voters to realize that elections do function to rid the institution of some of its worst offenders. The point, however, is that

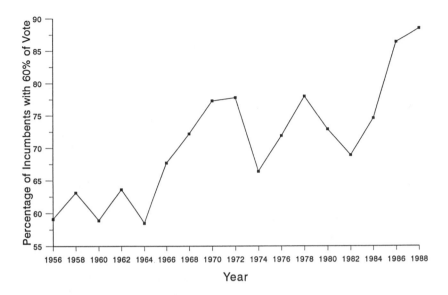

Fig. 5. House elections won by 60 percent of the vote, 1956–88. (From Ornstein, Mann, and Malbin 1990, 59.)

these transgressions must be uncovered and few inside and outside of Congress have incentives to do so. Legislators do not delve into the affairs of their colleagues with any relish, and the invisibility of the actions of most members prevents adequate monitoring of legislator behavior.

Even if ethical transgressions are uncovered, will the exposé be sufficient to uproot an entrenched incumbent? On occasion, yes, but generally speaking the high levels of electoral safety that characterize most incumbent election victories mean that only strong voter revolts will be effective. If an incumbent is in trouble at home for a variety of reasons, revelation of ethical transgressions may be adequate to deprive him or her of the increment of support necessary to retain the congressional seat. But highly popular incumbents will be another story. For one thing, the intense personal commitment of those in a legislator's electoral following serves to "screen out" the charges leveled against a beloved legislator; hence, electoral support will not quickly wither away. In short, dissonance-reducing rationales may develop among those loyal to a legislator that prevent ethical transgressions from negating existing voter commitments.

Moreover, even if ethical transgressions reach the ears of voters, there is no assurance that an adequate replacement will be found! The electoral strength of most incumbents scares off the types of candidates who wage competitive races. Voters are more familiar with incumbents than challengers and like incumbents more; and voters have many more contacts with incumbents than those who challenge them. Is it any wonder that recruiting challengers under such circumstances is akin to asking someone not only to join a losing cause but also to finance and lead it! Is it at all surprising that it is extremely difficult to find able politicians willing to contest the elections of incumbents?

Economists point to "monitoring" as an effective way to constrain opportunistic behavior, but wealth-maximizing legislators have little to fear: monitoring is rather infrequent or sporadic and legislators exercise considerable control over the release of information about themselves. High costs are incurred in gathering information about incumbents, and few local media (who would be most sensitive to the actions of the district representative) can afford the costs. Thus, most legislators escape monitoring because those who have the greatest interest in a representative's actions, like the local press and district voters, cannot afford the costs associated with monitoring legislative behavior. Those who can afford the costs—national media—rarely have incentives to scrutinize the behavior of individual incumbents.

Moreover, most of what voters hear and read about their own legislator has its genesis in the representative's own congressional office, which supplies information tailored to the legislator's preferences, not the voters'. This information is supplied to local media who then report it as if they had researched the story themselves. This symbiotic relationship—legislators want favorable local press and the local press wants news from Washington to impress its readers—assures that the incumbent is seen in the most favorable light. So, if incumbents cannot escape monitoring for some reason, they remain in a good position to influence the content of news reports about them. Therefore, rent-seeking politicians need not be overly concerned that their self-interest will be uncovered: few media sources are likely to concentrate their resources on monitoring their actions, and if some transgressions are uncovered, incumbents have access to channels of information that can be manipulated to give a more lenient, if not favorable, "spin" to the facts.

One important reason why existing controls on legislators are so weak is because there is a milieu within Congress that promotes mutual noninterference. That is, legislators are discouraged from interfering in the affairs of other members, and everyone benefits from being left alone. Legislators are normally *forced* to reprimand their colleagues, and they often seek the softest of penalties when they have to take action against another colleague. Members who sit in judgment—for instance, those on the Standards of Official Conduct Committee—serve only as a favor to their party leaders, not out of choice. This milieu is fostered by the existence of two norms that promote mutual noninterference among legislators: specialization and reciprocity.

The specialization norm not only assures some useful division of labor within the legislature but also discourages legislators from questioning the motives of specialists—they are assumed to know more about the issues involved than others. Hence, the specialization norm gives rent-extracting politicians a rationale for creating legislation and regulations relevant to those industries in their area of specialization. The reciprocity norm—assistance or favors rendered by another legislator should be paid in kind—also reduces the incentives to scrutinize the motives and actions of others by placing a high value on cooperation. Legislators are encouraged to help one another to facilitate the passage of legislation. Since every transaction reflects the self-interest of the parties involved, no one reaps any benefit by exposing another's preference to public ridicule. If a potential trading partner feels some moral indignation over what is being demanded, he or she need not carry out the exchange. Hence, legislators voice their disapproval by not trading support rather than by calling public attention to the bargain. This assures some anonymity to the actions of wealth-seeking legislators or at the very least reduces the probability of exposure by one's colleagues—those in the best position to monitor behavior within the legislature.

Who Finds Congressional Service Attractive?

The characteristics of Congress and the esteem of the institution create conditions conducive to adverse selection by influencing the mixture of monetary and intrinsic returns available through a congressional career. The mixture is not invariant, and shifts in the blend alter the composition of Congress by making the institution more (or less) attractive to potential recruits and present incumbents. Those with stronger preferences for the financial rewards rather than the intrinsic returns associated with service in the legislature find Congress more attractive when the mixture favors material returns. In contrast, those preferring intrinsic returns, or valuing such returns more than the financial rewards, find congressional service more rewarding when the mixture favors the intrinsic returns to a legislative career. Thus, the prominence of certain returns helps to influence the kinds of individuals who are attracted to congressional service.

This relationship between the returns from congressional service and the types of individuals attracted to Congress is evident in the changes over time in the percentage of noncareer politicians—"political amateurs"—entering Congress. By assumption 2 from chapter 2, politicians preferring the intrinsic to the material rewards of officeholding establish long careers in office thereby forgoing the financial gain associated with employment in the private sector. I refer to these individuals as "career" politicians. Noncareer politicians are individuals who are *not* attracted to office by the prospects of establishing long careers in politics. Political amateurs may occupy that status not out of a lack of interest in a political career but rather because they have never been successful in their attempts to obtain office. Unfortunately, the data do not allow for such delineations. Therefore, amateurs are equated with noncareer politicians in this analysis because of an inability to differentiate within the data among prospective career "amateurs" and those with little interest in establishing congressional careers. The term, however, is meant to describe only those who show no long-term commitment to public service rather than political novices with a history of unsuccessful attempts at officeholding.[3]

Figure 6 shows the trend in the percentage of freshman legislators without prior officeholding experience (i.e., noncareer politicians) who entered the House of Representatives between 1788 and 1990. For the first 140 years of the Republic (until 1930), less than 20 percent of the cohorts entering Congress over this period lacked experience in holding a local, state, or federal office. The percentage of political novices increases to 25 percent between 1930 and 1950 but declines to a mere 6 percent for nearly a quarter of a century (1952–74). As dramatic as this decline is, it is also short-lived: between 1976 and 1990 the percentage of political amateurs rises to 22 percent.

There are, of course, benefits to the influx of political novices into Congress. Often, amateur politicians are less constrained by prior legislative agreements, existing norms ("rules of the game"), or congressional practices thereby making them more willing to entertain innovation and reform and to challenge the status quo. While I do not deny the value of political amateurs, as I discussed in chapter 2, I believe that they also pose significant problems for the operation of a legislature *in a rent-seeking society*. In short, I do not feel that we can gain much solace from any upturn in the percentage of amateur politicians entering Congress.

---

3. This attribute—limited interest in establishing a career in politics—is an important difference between career and noncareer politicians. While all noncareer politicians can be described as "amateurs," not all amateurs are noncareer politicians since some amateurs aspire to establish political careers.

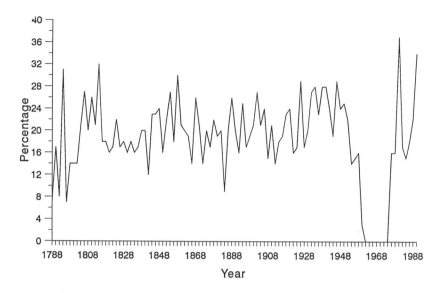

Fig. 6. House Freshmen without prior office experience, 1788–1990. (Data from ICPSR Study No. 7803.)

I have argued that the returns from congressional service incorporate both intrinsic and material rewards. Clearly, the political system in general, and Congress in particular, benefits from politicians attracted to office more by the intrinsic than the material rewards of officeholding. If the intrinsic rewards from congressional service diminish in response to losses in institutional esteem and increased rent seeking in the legislature, however, potential recruits attracted to office by these intrinsic returns—career politicians—will shun congressional office. Thus, fluctuations in the entry of career politicians into Congress should respond to the availability of these intrinsic returns.[4] I expect career politicians to be attracted to office by the high esteem of the institution and the longevity of a career in Congress. For individuals preferring the intrinsic

4. It might be suggested that the entrance of amateurs reflects voter decisions as much as self-recruitment; hence, the entrance of amateurs reflects voter preferences for noncareer politicians. The election of amateurs is not solely an expression of citizen contempt for politics and politicians in general: no matter how little institutions and officials are respected, esteemed politicians retain their public approbation in the worst of times. The public always prefers esteemed candidates, and well-respected politicians normally have little difficulty in defeating amateurs. Thus, the entrance of amateurs into Congress is not merely an electoral verdict but also reflects the decisions of career politicians not to seek congressional office (see, for instance, Canon 1990).

rewards of a political career such assets enhance the value of congressional service.

There are two additional reasons why we might expect noncareer politicians ("amateurs") to enter Congress in increasing proportions in response to declines in institutional esteem and increases in rent-seeking opportunities. First, since career politicians will find congressional service less attractive during periods when the institution is suffering from declining institutional esteem, the probability of a successful election increases for amateurs. Hence, low levels of institutional esteem provide fertile conditions for amateurs to launch their candidacies. The interest of career politicians in congressional office significantly reduces the likelihood that amateurs will be successful in obtaining office since experienced candidates will normally defeat inexperienced ones. Therefore, when amateurs win office it is generally because they were spared the task of running against an experienced opponent, all things being equal. (For an excellent treatment of the factors that induce amateurs to seek congressional office, see Canon 1990.) Second, the availability of rents assures noncareer politicians (amateurs) a large market for their services if elected; it also assures that amateurs will be able to find the type of campaign financing necessary to run a successful campaign. For these reasons, the factors that reduce the intrinsic returns to congressional service—declining institutional esteem and increases in the availability of rents—also serve to motivate noncareer politicians (amateurs) to seek and enter congressional service.

Although the data are fragile, these relationships do, indeed, have empirical validity. I have assembled data on the level of institutional esteem (congressional popularity),[5] career longevity (mean years of service among retirees),[6] and the potential for rent seeking (pages of federal regulations) to explain the fluctuations in the percentage of ama-

---

5. These data were obtained from the holdings of the Roper Public Opinion Research Center at the University of Connecticut and from Roger H. Davidson (for the years between 1965 and 1969). The tests of the adverse selection hypotheses will be necessarily crude due to the lack of unobtrusive information on the preferences of legislators— rational legislators have no incentives to reveal their true preferences for material gain. Therefore, I have relied upon the consistency in predictions deduced from the four assumptions in determining the validity of the hypotheses describing the consequences of adverse selection.

6. Historical data on the characteristics of members of Congress were obtained from the Inter-University Consortium for Political and Social Research: *Roster of United States Congressional Officeholders and Biographical Characteristics of Members of the United States Congress, 1789–1991* (ICPSR 7803). All historical data reported in this study were obtained from these data, unless specified otherwise.

teur politicians entering the House of Representatives.[7] These data span the years 1944 to 1990. The functional relationships can be modeled in the following manner:

$$A = f(U, C, R),\tag{2}$$

where,

> A = percentage of freshmen without prior officeholding experience at either the local, state, or federal levels,
> U = percentage of the electorate with unfavorable evaluations of congressional performance,
> C = mean years of House service at time of retirement,
> R = pages in the *Federal Register*.

Since career politicians prefer the intrinsic returns from a congressional career to the financial rewards, reductions in institutional esteem (i.e., increases in congressional unpopularity) reduce these returns and therefore the attractiveness of congressional service. Thus, the percentage of noncareer politicians entering Congress should increase as the *unpopularity* of Congress rises. The relationship between institutional esteem and the entrance of political amateurs is illustrated in figure 7 and appears consistent with this hypothesized effect.

Intrinsic returns also should be a function of career longevity: the longer the average congressional career, the greater the intrinsic returns expected from legislative service (assumption 2). Therefore, career politicians should be attracted to congressional service by the expected longevity of a career in Congress. It is, of course, impossible to determine a priori the longevity of a congressional career, but one indicator is the length of time legislators have served in Congress before retiring. Therefore, tenure at the time of retirement provides a crude indicator of the longevity that might be expected of a congressional career. Since intrinsic returns accumulate with tenure, office longevity (length of a congressional career) should make a congressional career attractive to those who relish the intrinsic rewards of officeholding. Thus, as the mean number of years of service of retirees increases, so should the proportion of career politicians entering the House.

---

7. Since I have defined career politicians as establishing long periods of public service, it would be preferable to have data on the actual length of public service rather than merely the number of levels of government served, as recorded in the data. Unfortunately, I have been unable to obtain such information for the purposes of this analysis.

Fig. 7. Congressional unpopularity and percentage of amateurs entering the House of Representatives, 1944–90. (Data compiled by author.)

The level of rent seeking in Congress is measured by the pages of federal regulations since regulations serve as a prominent means for *creating* rents (Stigler 1971; McChesney 1987). Stigler (1971) has argued that regulations provide economic interests with contrived market advantages thereby earning those interests supracompetitive profits—rents. Regulations also can be used to threaten groups to part with some of the economic profits they are earning (rent extraction) as the result of government inactivity or previous governmental actions (McChesney 1987). Finally, the existence of regulations provides opportunities for legislators to intervene in bureaucratic affairs and gain exemptions to these regulations or, in the name of "casework," see to it that interest groups obtain favorable agency interpretations of relevant regulations. Thus, the proliferation of regulations is a useful measure of the opportunities to engage in rent seeking in Congress. Pages of regulations serve as the indicator of potential rent-seeking opportunities.

In table 4 I present the OLS estimates obtained by regressing the percentage of freshman entering Congress without prior officeholding

TABLE 4. Explaining Changes in the Entry of Noncareer Politicians, 1944–90

Variables	Equation 1		Equation 2[a]	
	b	t-value	b	t-value
Pages in the *Federal Register* (per 100 pages) (R)	.0237	4.071**	.0266	3.000**
Mean years of service at retirement (C)	−2.1950	−3.312**	−.8583	−1.616*
Congressional unpopularity (U)	.6191	2.955**	.3828	2.412**
Statistics:				
N	19		19	
R^2	.59			
Adjusted R^2	.51			
Durbin-Watson statistic	1.175		2.350	

**$p \leq .01$
*$p \leq .10$
[a]This equation incorporates the Prais-Winsten method for correcting for autocorrelation. Other correction methods produced similar results.

experience, on the unpopularity of Congress, mean years of service among House retirees, and the number of pages in the *Federal Register*.[8] While the limited number of data points restricts the number of explanatory variables that can be safely analyzed, the model does not appear to be plagued by excessively large amounts of unexplained variation: 59 percent of the variation in the percentage of entering amateurs can be explained by this simple three-variable model. All of the statistical estimates are highly significant, and they are in the predicted directions. Rises in congressional unpopularity decrease the percentage of careerists entering Congress and the percentage of careerists also decreases with the growth in federal regulations. Increased tenure on the part of retirees, however, increases the percentage of career politicians entering the House.

These influences are not at all trivial (table 4, eq. 1): a 10 percent increase in congressional unpopularity increases the percentage of political novices entering the House by 6 percent, and a one-year increase in the mean number of years served by retirees *decreases* the percentage of political amateurs by 2 percent. Clearly, as the intrinsic returns from

8. Since the time series of congressional unpopularity has some missing data— namely, the years 1950, 1952, 1958, 1960, and 1962—the actual number of cases in the analysis is 19 instead of 24. The measurements of congressional unpopularity used in this analysis are the latest polls taken in each (available) odd-numbered year between 1944 and 1990. This was done to avoid any potential biasing effect of measuring congressional popularity during an election year or campaign.

congressional service diminish so does the proportion of career politicians entering the House.

One final point: the Durbin-Watson statistic in equation 1 is indecisive, giving us no assurance that a significant amount of autocorrelation is *not* biasing the interpretation of the coefficients. Equation 2 (table 4) presents the same equation but introduces the Prais-Winsten method to correct for the possible contaminating effects of autocorrelation. The findings are largely unchanged by the application of this correction: two of the three variables (pages of regulations and congressional unpopularity) retain their high levels of statistical significance. Career satisfaction (mean years of service at retirement), however, experiences a modest reduction in significance (.10 level of significance).

As mentioned earlier, one important consequence of a rent-seeking society is that a different set of skills becomes important, especially in legislatures. Normally, legal training, experience, and knowledge would be valued commodities in legislatures, given the preoccupation of such bodies with lawmaking. In a rent-seeking society, however, legislators gain by serving as middlemen to group-government transactions thereby extracting a piece of the pie for themselves. Thus, legal background may remain important, but the value of the skill for legislative service is no longer essential. If the rent-seeking society encourages prospective entrants to invest in those skills that best serve their own self-interest, legal training is clearly of declining value. This may explain the decrease in the percentage of lawyers entering Congress (fig. 8).

Similarly, having relatives who have served in Congress should also carry advantages for legislators and legislatures. Family members pass on a number of attributes that are beneficial to a legislature. Specifically, family members who have served in Congress can act in a tutorial capacity: knowledge is transmitted about the legislative processes (e.g., logrolling) and norms in the legislature (e.g., universalism). Here, too, there is an unmistakable decline in the percentage of entering freshmen who have relatives who have served in earlier congresses (fig. 9). As might be expected in the building of a nation, the early years of Congress had the greatest percentage of entering congressional cohorts with relatives having served in Congress. The trend begins a downward movement in the 1850s and follows an even steeper decline (single-digit percentages) in the early 1930s. Some of the lowest points in the series occur between 1970 and 1986. Like prior officeholding experience and legal training, having relatives who have served in Congress is less prevalent today than in the past. In sum, attributes that one might assume a priori to be important for effective service in Congress are not being

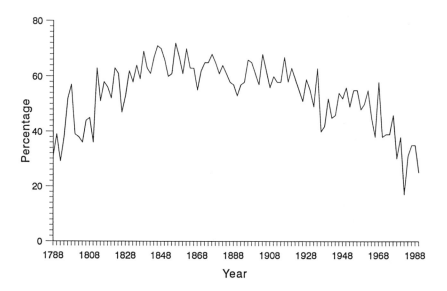

Fig. 8. House freshmen who are lawyers, 1788–90. (Data from ICPSR Study No. 7803.)

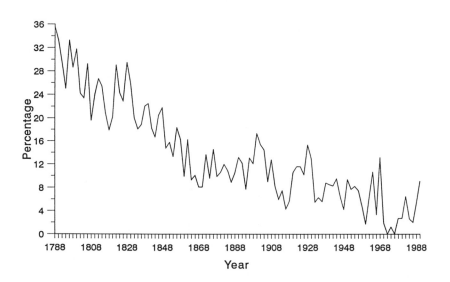

Fig. 9. Freshman legislators with relatives who have served in Congress, 1788–1990. (Data from ICPSR Study No. 7803.)

acquired by entering freshmen, and if the trends we have observed persist there are few reasons for prospective entrants to acquire these characteristics to hold legislative office.

Summary

The rent-seeking society has the capacity to afflict our institutions with the pernicious effects of adverse selection. As institutions become more accommodative to the rent-seeking behavior of their members, the character of these institutions changes and becomes more attractive to those interested in enhancing their personal wealth. If only those who appropriate rents are able to earn positive or satisfactory returns from their service in an institution, then "losers" (i.e., those who fail to earn positive profits through institutional service) will exit, and prospective recruits preferring nonmaterial returns will look elsewhere to invest their time and themselves. This could become a critical problem for Congress (if it is not one already) because at the same time the institution has gained attraction for individuals interested in financial gain it has lost attraction for those seeking intrinsic returns from a congressional career. I suspect that this is at least partially a consequence of the fact that the intrinsic returns from a congressional career are fading due to the low esteem accorded the job and the institution by the American public.

Congress appears to have lost attraction for career politicians in the sense that there has been an increase in the proportion of noncareer politicians entering the House since the early 1970s. This trend appears to respond to rises in the unpopularity of Congress, declines in career longevity, and increases in federal regulations. That is, the percentage of career politicians entering the House rises with increases in the popularity of Congress and the longevity of the congressional career. The growth in federal regulations, however, serves to decrease the proportion of careerists entering Congress. There are other indications of a decline in career politicians coming to Congress: the quality of House challengers has declined since the late 1980s (Jacobson 1990, 57–59); there has been a significant surge in the percentage of political amateurs entering the Senate between 1974 and 1982 (Canon 1990, 56–57); and there is evidence that some state legislators prefer to remain in the state house than run for Congress (Fowler and McClure 1989, 74–100). These findings, while consistent with the adverse selection hypotheses, are far too fragile to denounce Congress as composed entirely of rent seekers or even as having a critical mass of such legislators within the House. On the other hand, these results should make us apprehensive about the way in which the membership of Congress is presently evolving.

In sum, through the exiting of career politicians who can no longer earn satisfactory (positive) returns because of the low public esteem of Congress and the entrance of those who can earn positive returns in an unpopular institution (rent seekers), Congress may become populated by legislators who prefer the material to the intrinsic returns from a congressional career. While the empirical analysis is not without important caveats (e.g., limited number of observations, missing data), the relationships seem robust and in the predicted directions. The results suggest that the growth in rent-earning opportunities (federal regulations) and the possibility of serving in an unpopular institution deter career politicians from seeking congressional office. If the returns to a congressional career influence the type of individual entering the House, then the decline in the intrinsic returns of officeholding assures that entrants interested in these returns are more likely to shun legislative service, especially given the high costs of obtaining congressional office. Thus, the second adverse selection hypothesis gains support: rent-seeking activity in Congress decreases the attraction of the office to those who value highly the intrinsic returns of congressional service— namely, career politicians.

CHAPTER 5

Rent-Seeking Behavior in Congress

There are many ways in which rent-seeking behavior surfaces in Congress. In this chapter, I examine three political activities of legislators that can be linked to rent seeking: taking honoraria, spending large amounts on reelection campaigns, and obtaining campaign funds. Honoraria income, for instance, can serve as a form of quasilegal pay that provides a mechanism for groups to reward legislators who help them obtain preferential treatment from government. Similarly, campaign funds can serve as a vehicle for compensating legislators to assure that group interests are accommodated in the legislative process. Excessive campaign spending to obtain congressional office is consistent with what we would expect if the rents obtained through legislative membership exceeded those obtained in private employment. That is, the willingness of incumbents to spend large amounts of money in their reelection campaigns may reflect the capacity of the office to supply a high level of extralegal pay. This brief discussion should *not* be construed as suggesting that all honoraria, campaign spending, or fund-raising serve these rent-seeking purposes. My point is that while there is no assurance that these mechanisms will be subverted to serve the interests of rent-seeking legislators, there is also no guarantee that they cannot be used to this end.

A major objective of this chapter is to describe how the structure of Congress influences the rents earned by legislators. "Given politicians who are 'willing to be bought' through illegal bribes or legal campaign contributions," Susan Rose-Ackerman writes, "organizational factors will play a role in determining the volume of money which changes hands" (1978, 11). Unwittingly, perhaps, the hierarchical organization of Congress (especially the House of Representatives) and the absence of mechanisms for upholding legislator-group agreements have served to increase the monetary returns many legislators receive from their efforts to assist special interests through the legislative process. The hierarchical organization of the House of Representatives places some members in positions that enable them to perform services for groups at substantially lower costs than other legislators might require. Hence, those legislators who, because of institutional sources of influence, can supply the required service at the lowest cost gain the most business.

The absence of mechanisms to enforce agreements between legislators and groups—short of very risky efforts to thwart the reelection of entrenched incumbents—makes it necessary for groups to supply bonuses ("price premiums") to assure contractual compliance. Since there is no mechanism to assure that legislators actually do what groups ask of them or to punish them if they do not live up to their bargains, groups pay extra—beyond the actual cost of the service—to reward those who keep their agreements. Thus, there are organizational features of the House that influence the amount of quasilegal pay that legislators can collect. Such features make Congress an inviting target for rent seekers.

This chapter is also devoted to an examination of the third adverse selection hypothesis: recent generations of legislators engage in rent-seeking behavior to a greater degree than older congressional cohorts. More precisely, I analyze changes over time in two campaign activities that serve rent-seeking purposes: spending to obtain office and raising campaign war chests. If the "replacement hypothesis" (i.e., there is a generational change in rent-seeking behavior) is correct, recent congressional cohorts should engage in rent-seeking behavior to a greater extent than earlier generations.

How the Structure of Congress Influences the Rents Earned by Legislators

In a rent-seeking society, legislators earn the most by supplying political favors at the lowest cost and by upholding their agreements. The prices charged special interests for supplying some sort of preferential treatment vary depending upon the type of service—for instance, laws may be more expensive to supply than routine bureaucratic intercessions on behalf of group interests—but they are also influenced by the hierarchical organization of Congress and the absence of mechanisms for enforcing contracts. The structure of Congress places some individuals in strategic positions to influence the nature of public policy. For example, the Speaker and the majority and minority leaders in Congress have considerable say over the agenda of legislative business. Hence, these legislators can command very lucrative commissions for expediting business. Even though it might cost a lot to influence high-ranking congressional officers, the probability of legislative success is greater and therefore the expected payoff to the group is normally larger. No matter the price, it is undoubtedly less than other legislators would demand because institutional positions encompass powers and prerogatives that minimize the costs incurred in supplying special interest favors.

The structure of Congress also influences the price of legislator services by necessitating additional compensation to assure that legislators faithfully fulfill their agreements. As noted earlier, it is difficult to guarantee that a bargain is kept between a group and a legislator since there are no real mechanisms—outside of the unenviable and risky task of replacing a shirking legislator—to assure contractual compliance. While legislators may have an incentive to keep their agreements because of the desire to maintain their reputations (brand-name capital) and assure future business (repeat purchases), issues of moral hazard (for instance, the difficulty inherent in observing a legislator's efforts on a group's behalf) yield legislators considerable slack. For these reasons, groups pay a "price premium" to those who can be counted on to fulfill their side of a bargain. In the following pages, I show how the costs of service and the potential for legislator shirking (reneging on agreements) influenced the distribution of honoraria in the U.S. Congress in 1989.

In this segment of the study, the dependent variable is the amount of honoraria (in dollars) raised by senators and representatives in 1989, a nonelection year. Studies of the relationship between legislative behavior and interest-group money have usually centered on political action committee (PAC) contributions to the campaigns of incumbent legislators (see, for example, Gopoian 1984). Data on honoraria provide another important perspective on the question of interest-group payments to legislators. Little attention has been given to the payment of honoraria to incumbents because of the difficulty in obtaining information on the personal finances of senators and representatives and in identifying the actual dollar amounts received through honoraria. The recent availability of these data as a result of financial disclosure requirements provides a unique opportunity to explore an obvious example of quasilegal pay.

Honoraria have now been eliminated, but prior to this action there were legal limits to the amount of money that legislators were allowed to keep from earned honoraria: 30 percent of a representative's salary and 40 percent of a senator's salary. However, there were no limits to the amount *earned,* only the amount retained. Money in excess of these limits was required to be contributed to charity. Despite this charitable aspect to the raising of honoraria dollars, financial benefits still accrued to raising large sums of money because they enabled legislators to count these sums as income for purposes of increasing tax deductions. While any restraint on the income earned through honoraria might constrain rent extractions, many members still earned beyond the stipulated limit.

Since honoraria were scheduled to be eliminated entirely in the House and reduced in the Senate by about \$12,000 in 1991, legislators had strong incentives in 1989 to exploit existing opportunities for rent extractions because the future value of this quasilegal pay would decline rapidly in the next term of office. In short, sufficient incentives existed, at least in 1989, to encourage legislators to reveal their preferences for quasilegal, interest-group money.

Explanatory Variables. A variety of independent variables are included in this analysis of honoraria to illustrate the importance of the structure of Congress. *Low-cost suppliers of political favors* are characterized in this analysis as holding positions of influence in the institutional power structure within the House or Senate. A legislator's position in the legislature enables him or her to perform services at a lower cost than others: positions of influence entail resources, powers, and contacts that facilitate the types of exchanges essential for implementing group objectives. Thus, a legislator's position in the institutional structure influences the costs incurred in supplying political favors for groups. The "better" one's institutional position—the more influence ascribed to a position—the lower the cost of supplying political favors. Figure 10 illustrates the value of being a low-cost supplier of political favors.

Figure 10 describes four supply curves intersecting the demand for legislation; each supply curve represents the volume of legislation sup-

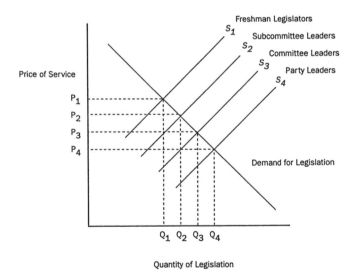

Fig. 10. Cost and supply of legislation

plied and the cost associated with each curve. The supply curves to the left (S_1, S_2, and S_3) entail greater opportunity costs than S_4. For instance, let us assume a particular group wants a bill enacted into law. Any legislator can supply the law but the costs of doing so will vary according to the institutional position of the legislator. For example, a freshman legislator will incur higher costs in enacting the legislation than, say, a party or committee leader. The latter are positioned to facilitate the exchanges necessary to pass the specified legislation. They have earned favors ("chits") as a result of their ability to help others, largely due to their positions of institutional power. The more powerful the legislator, the greater the number of legislators indebted or obligated to him or her—factors that facilitate the passage of legislation beneficial to clientele interests.

Thus, the supply curve for party leaders rests below the curves for committee and subcommittee leaders. The supply curve for freshmen legislators requires the greatest cost and, assuming a competitive return, necessitates a higher price. Under these conditions, groups should seek out those legislators with the lowest prices for their services—i.e., those with the lowest costs of supply. In short, low-cost suppliers (those in positions of institutional power) obtain the largest honoraria incomes. In the smaller Senate, there are considerably fewer suppliers of political favors than in the House. Hence, senators should obtain higher prices than representatives for their services. Figure 11 illustrates this hypothetical relationship.

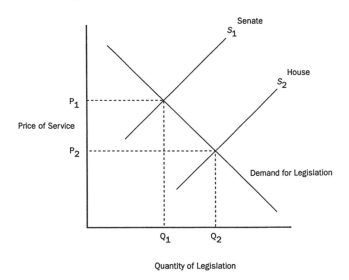

Fig. 11. Cost and supply of legislation in the House and Senate

To maximize their returns, groups seek out low-cost suppliers who therefore do the most business and obtain the greatest quasilegal incomes. Here I consider three measures of institutional power: membership in the party leadership, seniority ranking, and assignment to important legislative committees. I measure a legislator's position in the institutional power structure according to whether he or she is a committee or party leader: Senate majority leader, Senate majority whip, chair of the Democratic Conference in the Senate, Senate minority leader, assistant Senate minority leader, chair of the Republican Conference in the Senate, Speaker of the House, House majority leader, House majority whip, chairman of the Democratic Caucus in the House, House minority leader, House minority whip, and chairman of the Republican Conference in the House. These offices constitute the highest levels of institutional influence followed by chairmanships of standing committees and chairmanships of subcommittees (of the standing committees). Seniority ranking is merely a legislator's position within the seniority hierarchy (i.e., the greater a legislator's seniority, the lower his or her ranking).

The taxing committees in the House and Senate (Ways and Means and Finance, respectively) play a central role in the legislative process. These committees supply direct economic benefits, such as tax loopholes to groups and individuals. Thus, membership on the House Ways and Means or the Finance Committee in the Senate places legislators in important positions to help clientele interests or to help other legislators not on these committees serve the interests of important groups within their own constituencies. Legislators holding such positions of institutional power are expected to serve group interests at lower costs than those legislators not similarly advantaged. As a result, they—those in positions of institutional power—gain more "business" and therefore have higher (honoraria) incomes.

I also assume that price premiums are paid by groups to assure legislator support. The price premium is over and above the price of the service supplied and is paid to legislators who can be counted upon to fulfill their agreements—a form of "protection money" (see Klein and Leffler 1981). The more reliable the legislator, the higher the premium he receives. Since business rather than labor groups incur lower costs in mobilizing supporters and overcoming organizational obstacles to lobbying (Olson 1965), business groups can better afford to offer price premiums to legislators who deliver on their promises.[1] Finally, the potential

---

1. There is no significant relationship between legislator support of labor policies as rated by the AFL-CIO and honoraria income. Hence, this variable is not included in the final equations in the analysis.

for shirking (reneging on promises and agreements) is measured by whether or not a legislator has announced his or her intention to resign. The incentive for shirking should be greatest for legislators in their last term of office since these legislators have little to fear from group reprisals at the next election. The possibility of "repeat purchases"—future business—is lost along with the corresponding incentive to live up to one's promises.

These relationships can be defined in the following manner:

$$H = f(S, T, P, R, B),\tag{3}$$

where

H = amount of honoraria income earned in 1989,
S = seniority ranking,
T = membership on a committee with responsibility for tax legislation,
P = position in institutional power structure,
R = legislator has announced an intention to retire,
B = business ratings of the voting records of legislators.

Analysis. The first point I should make is that senators have higher honoraria incomes than representatives (mean level of $29,215). The greater earning power of senators is consistent with the hypothesis that the smaller size of the Senate relative to the House of Representatives results in fewer suppliers of political favors. Hence, senators receive a higher income from their sales. Also consistent with the notion of fewer suppliers in the Senate is the fact that since the 1940s the House has historically maintained at least a two to one edge over the Senate in the number of bills introduced. Thus, due to the limited number of suppliers, rents in the Senate are higher and bill production is lower than in the House.

It is clear from both of the equations (House and Senate) that low-cost suppliers of political favors collect the greatest amount of honoraria (table 5): membership in the leadership structure or on a tax committee (House equation only) yields significant rents. In the House, each rung in the institutional power structure is worth about $7,500 ($b = 7,480.04$) so that committee leaders on the average pocket about $15,000, and membership on Ways and Means earns House members over $20,000 ($b = 20,254.58$). In the Senate, membership on the Finance Committee is worth considerably less, about $7,000 ($b = 7,031.61$), but each rung in the ladder of power ($b = 10,388.85$) is worth 50 percent more than in the House.

TABLE 5. Important Determinants of the Distribution in Honoraria Income among Members of Congress, in Dollars

Variables	House	Senate
Seniority rank (S)	−48.69	59.72
	(−2.78)	(.39)
Membership on tax committee (T)	20254.58	7031.61
	(5.23)	(1.34)
Position in institutional structure (P)	7480.04	10388.85
	(3.90)	(3.73)
Retiring member (R)	1141.97	−23299.15
	(.26)	(−2.31)
Chamber of Commerce rating (B)	−14.34	639.78
	(−.35)	(6.35)
Statistics:		
Multiple R	.41	.60
R^2	.16	.36
Adjusted R^2	.15	.33
N	409	93
F-statistic	15.79	9.99

Note: Unstandardized regression coefficients; *t*-values in parentheses below coefficients.

In the House, seniority proves to be an asset, symptomatic of what we expect of low-cost suppliers—the higher a legislator is in the seniority hierarchy (the lower his or her seniority ranking) the more money is earned through honoraria. In the Senate, however, tenure has no significant effect on a legislator's earnings from honoraria.[2] Legislator support for the interests of business, as rated by the U.S. Chamber of Commerce, earns a senator a sizable premium—over $600 ($b = 639.78$) for each percentage point increase in group support. However, price premiums appear insignificant relative to the amount of honoraria collected by House incumbents.

Some of these contrasting results can be explained by institutional and organizational differences between the House and Senate. For instance, the widespread dispersal of power in the Senate—virtually every

2. This difference in the impact of seniority on interest-group money in the House and Senate is also observed in the distribution of PAC contributions (Grier and Munger 1993). It might appear that the relationship between honoraria income and seniority is evidence that increased tenure does not slow rent-seeking behavior. Seniority represents both power and longevity, but it is the element of power in seniority that matters most to the honoraria income of legislators. The inability of seniority to increase honoraria income in the Senate, where seniority means little to individual power, is consistent with the notion that the relationship between seniority and honoraria income reflects the significance of power in reducing the costs involved in serving special interests.

member of the majority party holds a position of institutional power—reduces the value of seniority as a determinant of legislative power. Similarly, membership on the Finance Committee is less valuable as a position of Senate power than is membership on the Ways and Means Committee within the House power structure, possibly because tax legislation originates in the House.

Perhaps the most interesting differences in the earnings of House and Senate incumbents relate to the greater impact of retirement and support for the legislative interests of business groups on the honoraria incomes of senators. In the House, neither of these variables attains statistical significance. These differences, I believe, are the result of the higher costs of doing business in the Senate. As a consequence of these higher costs, groups assume more risk in their dealings with senators. The major risk from the perspective of interest groups is shirking, and where the costs are high so are the risks for such groups. In these circumstances, groups are willing and prepared to pay price premiums to assure contractual performance. That is, groups are willing to pay *extra* for assurance that a senator will not shirk. Therefore, extra payment for supporting business interests is more likely to occur in the Senate because the costs and the risks are quite high.

This premise also explains the significance of retirements to the earning power of senators. Retiring senators are poor contractual risks because the potential period of shirking is unusually long—six years—unlike the House with its two-year term. Hence, assurance that a member will continue in office for at least another term is worth more in the Senate than the House. Here again, the higher costs of legislative service in the Senate make groups more willing to pay extra for quality assurances—assurances that legislators will not engage in postcontractual opportunism. Thus, an announcement of retirement costs a senator dearly—over $23,000! Price premiums are less necessary to assure contractual performance in the House because the "repurchase" period (i.e., term of office) is shorter (two years) than in the Senate with its six-year term. The shorter repurchase period reduces the incentives for cheating (Klein and Leffler 1981) and also the willingness of groups to supply extra pay for assurance against legislator shirking.

In sum, low-cost suppliers of political favors receive the highest honoraria incomes. The wider dispersal of power in the Senate as compared to the House reduces the effects of seniority and membership on the Finance Committee in determining institutional influence. Hence, these variables are significantly related to honoraria income only in the House. The smaller the number of suppliers in the Senate relative to the House means that senators obtain higher prices for their

services. Business groups also are more willing to pay senators extra—
a price premium—to assure that no shirking occurs.[3] The major conclusions drawn from the above analysis illustrate a basic premise of this
study: the structure of Congress is quite accommodative to the interests
of wealth-maximizing legislators.

Explaining Over-Time Changes in Rent Seeking

Another facet of the adverse selection argument is that changes in rent-
seeking behavior over time are generational in nature. That is, adverse
selection may have resulted in an increased penchant for rent seeking on
the part of recent cohorts entering the House. The characteristics of
Congress that facilitate rent seeking (e.g., lack of monitoring, decentralization), and the erosion of institutional esteem and the intrinsic returns
from a congressional career, may have altered the composition of Congress so that rent seekers, rather than career politicians, now find legislative service most rewarding. If this assumption is correct, we can expect
recent generations of legislators to engage in more rent-seeking activity
than past generations. That is, recent generations should raise more
campaign money and spend far more on their reelection campaigns than
older generations of legislators. Such conditions do not bode well for
Congress: if left unchecked, the institution could become little more
than a mechanism for facilitating rent seeking. Ideally, this state of
affairs is constrained in a natural way: the increased value of the intrinsic
returns to officeholding and the diminishing productive nature of rent
seeking should limit rent-seeking behavior.

As noted earlier, the effort to produce rents experiences a decline in
marginal productivity with time, but intrinsic returns increase in value as
the force of seniority elevates legislators to positions of institutional and
national prominence (assumption 3 from chapter 2). Since rent seeking
reduces the intrinsic returns of the job (assumption 4), legislators must
choose whether to invest more effort in producing rents or in consuming
the intrinsic rewards (e.g., taking statesmanlike policy positions, developing national policies). The decision may be a difficult one, but it gets
much easier with time because increased effort in rent seeking will eventually be "unproductive" while the intrinsic returns from the job rise.
Most utility-maximizing legislators should opt for increased consump-

---

3. There is no evidence that being a lawyer, acquiring a large number of committee
assignments, receiving high ratings by labor unions, representing a safe district, or introducing numerous legislative bills increases one's honoraria income in any significant way
(Parker 1992b).

tion of the intrinsic benefits of the job, especially those who realize the virtue of a long career in Congress—and the longer they stay, the greater the appreciation! Therefore, just as career politicians must like every legislator engage in some sort of rent seeking to protect constituents' interests, even rent-seeking legislators come to appreciate the value of a congressional career with time: the marginal productivity of rent-seeking behavior declines, but the consumption of the intrinsic returns increases in attractiveness. Rent seeking increases until the marginal gain in the production of rents is less than the marginal value of the intrinsic returns sacrificed through increased rent seeking.

Thus, both generational and seniority effects can be expected to influence levels of rent seeking in Congress: newer generations of legislators should engage in rent-seeking activities to a greater degree than older cohorts, but such behavior should decline as legislators gain seniority. At first glance, the argument for adverse selection might end here. After all, if rent seekers become less so with time, we really have nothing to worry about: the longer rent seekers are in Congress, the fewer incentives they have to intensify or expand their rent-seeking behavior. The argument could be halted at this point if it were not for the proviso added to the assumption that the intrinsic returns from officeholding increase with time—namely, "all things being equal."

While rent-seeking legislators come to appreciate the intrinsic returns from legislative service with seniority, the rate at which they shift their efforts from the investment in rent-earning endeavors to the consumption of the intrinsic rewards of officeholding will slow during periods when these intrinsic returns are in decline, for example, if Congress is held in low public regard. Declines in public confidence and respect for Congress diminish the intrinsic returns to officeholding, depreciating the marginal gain sacrificed through increased rent-seeking efforts. As table 6 demonstrates, confidence in Congress is quite low—about one of every five voters has "hardly any" confidence in those running the institution. Moreover, the ranks of the least trusting (those with "hardly any" confidence in Congress) have swelled since 1977, although not in a monotonic fashion. Declining public esteem may not completely negate the effects of seniority in tempering the rent-seeking behavior of legislators, but it undoubtedly weakens the effectiveness of this control. This explains why some rent-seeking politicians never seem to shift their efforts over time.

When institutional esteem is low or declining, the intrinsic returns from officeholding are discounted at a higher rate. This makes rent seeking a more attractive activity thereby reducing the incentives for legislators to shift their efforts to the consumption of the intrinsic

TABLE 6. Confidence in Congress

Question: "I am going to name some institutions in this country. As far as the people running these institutions are concerned, would you say you have a great deal of confidence, only some confidence, or hardly any confidence at all?"

Level of Confidence	1973	1974	1975	1976	1977	1978	1980	1982	1983	1984	1986	1987	1988	1989	1990	1991
A great deal	24	17	13	14	19	13	9	13	10	13	16	16	15	17	15	18
Only some	59	59	59	58	61	63	53	62	64	64	61	63	62	58	59	54
Hardly any	15	21	25	26	17	21	34	22	23	22	20	18	19	22	23	26
Don't know	3	3	3	3	3	3	4	2	3	2	3	3	3	3	3	3
N	1,497	1,481	1,487	1,494	1,523	1,527	1,466	1,501	1,592	976	1,465	1,463	995	1,537	1,472	1,517

Source: General Social Surveys, National Opinion Research Center, University of Chicago, 1973–91.

rewards of legislative service. As the intrinsic returns to officeholding decline, it is difficult to convince rent-seeking legislators that their efforts to produce rents result in the sacrifice of valuable intrinsic rewards. In sum, the rent-seeking society affects the willingness of legislators to substitute the consumption of the intrinsic returns to congressional service for the production of rents. Rent-seeking behavior, by reducing the intrinsic rewards to a legislative career, diminishes the influence of seniority in constraining legislators' appetites for rents. Thus, it is unlikely that the rent-seeking activities of House members will exhibit strong seniority effects: that is, declines in rent-seeking behavior during the course of a congressional career.

Methodology. The analysis of the campaign finances of House incumbents necessitates a cohort analysis of legislators' campaign receipts and expenditures. Cohort analysis involves the problem of separating cohort, period, and seniority effects—a problem often ignored in contemporary studies of over-time change even though such a neglect could produce dubious, if not fallacious, arguments and conclusions. The problem arises frequently when scholars obtain measurements of differing behaviors that are either cross-sectional or longitudinal in nature. Researchers either measure the differences between cohorts at the same point in time (i.e., cross-sectional differences) or differences within the same cohort over time (i.e., longitudinal differences). Inferences based upon cross-sectional differences cannot, by themselves, differentiate between seniority and cohort effects, nor can inferences from longitudinal comparisons distinguish between seniority and period effects. This is not merely the result of data limitations; the separation of generational, seniority, and period effects is only possible under certain conditions. In the following pages, I describe the conditions necessary for separating these effects. My methodological approach has been guided by the research strategy developed by sociologist Erdman Palmore (1978) for separating cohort, period, and seniority effects. This method has proved quite useful in analyzing changes over time in other forms of congressional behavior (see, for example, Parker 1986, 72–85).

Differences in campaign expenditures and receipts—two political activities linked to rent seeking—can be measured in three ways: as longitudinal, cross-sectional, or time-lag differences. Longitudinal differences are those observed between earlier and later measurements of the expenditures or receipts of members of a single congressional cohort. Cross-sectional differences are those between the expenditures (or receipts) of older and younger cohorts at the same point in time. Finally, time-lag differences are those between the expenditures (or receipts) of an older cohort after a certain period of time in the House of Representatives and later measurements of the campaign financial activity of younger cohorts after the same period of tenure. Each observable difference is related to two effects: age (seniority) effects result in longitudinal and cross-sectional differences; period effects produce longitudinal and time-lag differences; cohort effects create cross-sectional and time-lag differences (Palmore 1978, 285). This explains why valid inferences cannot be made on the basis of any single type of observed difference: each observable difference is composed of two possible effects. Patterns among these differences can provide, however, evidence that helps to distinguish the impact of one influence from that of another.

There are three basic patterns of observable differences that can be obtained: no significant differences, two significant differences, and three significant differences. The significance of the differences in campaign expenditures and receipts can be identified on the basis of their statistical probability (i.e., statistical tests of significance). If longitudinal, cross-sectional, and time-lag differences in campaign expenditures (receipts) are not significantly different from what might be expected on the basis of chance alone, the reasonable inference is that there is no evidence of generational (cohort), period, or seniority effects underlying changes in expenditures (receipts).

If two of the three differences are statistically significant, then one is justified in inferring that only a single effect is present and manifested in the existence of two types of significant differences. The identification of the single effect that underlies the two types of differences can be made by observing which effect is common to the two significant differences (table 7). Inferences are the most problematic when all three differences are present. That is, if cross-sectional, longitudinal, and time-lag differences in campaign spending activity (raising revenue and making expenditures) appear, individual effects cannot be separated without an additional assumption—namely, that one of the three effects is unlikely to be present. In order to discount the influence of one of the three effects, additional information will need to be examined to justify

TABLE 7. Measuring and Observing Seniority, Cohort, and Period Effects

	Type of Difference		
Effect	Longitudinal	Cross-sectional	Time-Lag
Seniority	X	X	
Cohort		X	X
Period	X		X

the exclusion of one of the effects. The statistical significance of the differences is based on t-tests and F-tests (ANOVA).

Changes Over Time in Campaign Receipts and Expenditures

As mentioned earlier, campaign receipts and expenditures can be construed as expressions of rent seeking. For example, campaign revenue may reflect side payments to legislators for past and future service, and campaign expenditures may reflect the overspending that accompanies competition for offices where the extralegal pay is considerable. Unfortunately, these campaign finance activities are on the rise (fig. 12 and 13). These trends in campaign spending activity can be linked to the impact of a rent-seeking society.

One way in which rent seeking can account for the changes over time in campaign receipts and expenditures (fig. 12 and 13) is through adverse selection. Through the entrance of politicians placing a higher value on the material benefits of legislative office and the exit of those who prefer intrinsic returns, generational changes in Congress may result in increased rent seeking. Thus, the entrance of recent cohorts who prefer the monetary rewards of congressional service to the intrinsic returns may produce a generational replacement that has increased rent-seeking behavior in Congress.

Increased campaign spending and revenue raising also could be characterized as being at least partially a product of a "period" effect: the entrenchment of a rent-seeking society. The rent-seeking milieu that increasingly characterizes legislator-special interest interactions reduces the esteem of Congress thereby reducing the intrinsic returns to legislative service; precipitates defensive rent seeking on the part of those who are disinclined to do so; and undermines the effects of seniority that normally increases the consumption of the intrinsic rewards of congressional service thereby reducing rent-seeking behavior by senior legislators.

Rent seeking reduces the esteem of Congress by encouraging illegal and/or unethical behavior that often creates scandals. Unfortunately, most legislators find themselves involved in rent seeking because it is a necessary means to serve constituency groups, to ensure that constituency interests are protected against the rent-seeking activity of other legislators, and to obtain funds to keep ahead of the rising costs of holding an office that yields considerable extra-legislative pay. Finally, rent seeking impairs the functioning of seniority—a mechanism that ideally constrains rent-seeking behavior. I have argued that the

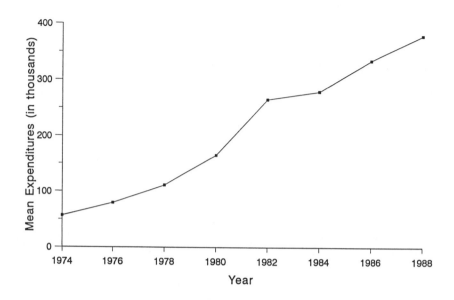

Fig. 12. Campaign expenditures by House incumbents, 1974–88. (Data from Ornstein, Mann, and Malbin 1990, 71.)

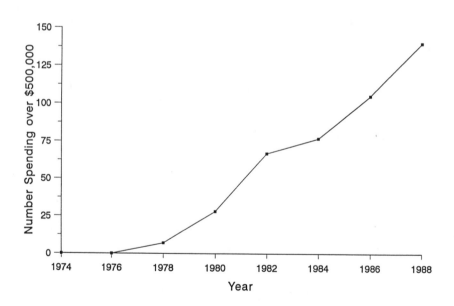

Fig. 13. Overspending for congressional office by House candidates, 1974–88. (Data from Ornstein, Mann, and Malbin 1990, 74.)

consumption of the intrinsic returns of legislative careers normally rises with tenure. However, rent seeking creates conditions that decrease the value of these returns thereby diminishing the intrinsic returns sacrificed through increased rent seeking. Thus, if legislators seek to maximize their utility, they either engage in rent seeking for a longer duration, and/or they increase rather than decrease their rent-seeking activities as they gain seniority. That is, there is reason to believe that the effect of the rent-seeking society in reducing the intrinsic returns to congressional service has rendered the impact of seniority ineffective in constraining rent seeking. In short, given the nature of the rent-seeking society, I doubt a seniority constraint persists. If it did, rent-seeking behavior within Congress would not evidence such a spiraling growth (fig. 12 and 13). In sum, it is unlikely that increases over time in campaign receipts and expenditures can be explained by the dynamics of increasing tenure since seniority should *depress,* not increase, rent-seeking behavior. Thus, I do not expect that seniority operates to constrain the growth in rent-seeking behavior in Congress. I will have more to say about the seniority hypothesis when the data are examined in the next section.

The data for this segment of the analysis are based upon the campaign expenditure and receipts of House members elected before 1984 who remained in office throughout the 1982–90 period. Hence, the data consist of a panel of congressional incumbents. I have defined congressional cohorts on the basis of the year they entered Congress, except for the two earliest cohorts (i.e., those elected before 1966 and those elected between 1968 and 1972) to assure an adequate number of cases for within-cohort analyses (longitudinal differences in expenditures and receipts). Finally, I have adjusted the figures for campaign receipts and expenditures by the GNP deflator for each particular election year (in 1982 dollars).[4] This assures that whatever increases are observed in receipts and expenditures are not merely due to rises in inflation.

Analysis of campaign expenditures. Table 8 describes the mean level of campaign expenditures by House incumbents elected prior to 1984, organized by election period and year of entry into the House of Representatives (cohorts). In every election period, the oldest cohort of representatives spent considerably less than legislators elected since 1976, and during two of the four election periods (i.e., 1981–82 and 1983–84) the youngest cohort spent more on their campaigns than all other cohorts. The relationship is not completely monotonic, however. For example,

---

4. The GNP deflator for each year is as follows: 1982 = 100; 1984 = 107.7; 1986 = 113.8; 1988 = 113.8; 1990 = 131.5.

the 1968–72 cohort spent more than younger cohorts in several instances and those elected in 1976 spent some of the lowest amounts on their campaigns. Despite such inconsistencies, the generational differences in campaign expenditures are statistically significant in three of the election periods during the decade (i.e., 1981–82, 1983–84, and 1987–88). Thus, cross-sectional differences in campaign expenditures can be observed.

Table 8 also reveals the existence of significant longitudinal differences within every cohort except the most recent cohort (i.e., 1982). In six of the cohorts, campaign spending increased significantly during the ten-year period; all of these changes occurred after 1984. Even though the oldest cohort of legislators decreased their expenditures in two of the election periods, campaign spending in 1985–86 and 1989–90 remained higher than in the two earliest election periods (i.e., 1981–82, 1983–84). In short, with the exception of the most recent generation of representatives, all cohorts experienced increased spending on their campaigns during the 1980s. It is unclear why the most recent generation (i.e., those elected in 1982) exhibited no significant change in spending during the ten-year period of study. Perhaps their declining level of spending is a regression-to-the-mean effect, where extreme observations tend to become less so with successive measurement. This cohort (1982) spent considerably more than other generations in their first elections as incumbent officeholders, and only the highest level of spending recorded by any cohort (those elected between 1968 and 1972) rivaled their campaign expenditures in their second terms, 1985–86. Hence, the most recent cohort displayed extremely high levels of campaign spending in their early years. Under such conditions, a decline in expenditures is not so unexpected.

TABLE 8.   Mean Level of Campaign Expenditures by House Cohorts, 1981–90, in 1982 Dollars

Election Period	1966 or Before	1968–72	1974	1976	1978	1980	1982
1981–82**	204,220	259,380	204,250	165,782	209,908	331,452	
1983–84**	165,887	267,963	236,879	202,120	251,929	242,466	305,291
1985–86	228,381*	320,847[a]	250,292	223,417[a]	267,082[a]	269,087	285,545
1987–88**	186,010[a]	295,822	320,511*	253,101[a]	310,945*	302,098[a]	269,212
1989–90	239,413*	303,522	308,122[a]	274,334[a]	326,467[a]	278,882	269,133
N	37	32	29	29	33	40	65

Source: Federal Election Commission Reports 1981–90.
*Statistically significant at .05 level: longitudinal difference (one-tailed test).
**Statistically significant at .05 level: cross-sectional difference.
[a]Significant longitudinal difference between this mean and nonadjacent mean for this cohort.

Further evidence of generational effects in campaign expenditures can be found in the time-lag differences in expenditures (table 9). Cohort differences persist when attention is given to the expenditures of cohorts at the same points in their congressional careers. While the time-lag differences are somewhat less significant than the cross-sectional differences in campaign expenditures (table 8), the pattern is similar: more recent cohorts (i.e., those elected after 1978) spent more on their campaigns than older generations at the same point in their legislative careers in the House. For example, after three terms (six years), those elected in 1976 spent an average of $100,000 less on their campaigns than those entering Congress in 1980 and 1982. There is little evidence that the campaign spending of more recent generations of legislators eventually resembles that of earlier cohorts with the passage of time.

The existence of all three differences complicates the interpretation of these data by requiring the elimination of one of the three effects—seniority, period, or cohort. I have eliminated the possibility of seniority effects for the following reasons. First, increased seniority is expected to decrease rent-seeking behavior by increasing the consumption of the intrinsic benefits of officeholding. However, in every cohort (except those elected in 1982) campaign spending increased—even among the most senior legislators. Second, it could be argued that increased spending should be related to rising seniority: since increased tenure is associated with positions of institutional influence and power, the capacity to extract rents should also increase. Hence, legislators can be expected to increase the rents earned as they gain seniority. From this perspective, seniority effects imply increased rents and therefore predict *increases* over time in campaign expenditures. If this is true, senior members should be spending and receiving *more* campaign funds than junior legislators. However, the relationships are just the opposite—junior

TABLE 9. Time-lag Differences in Campaign Expenditures among Cohorts, in 1982 Dollars

Years Served	1982	1980	1978	1976
2	305,291	331,452		
4*	285,545	242,466	209,908	
6*	269,212	269,087	251,929	165,782
8[a]	269,133	302,098	267,082	202,120
N	65	40	33	29

Source: Federal Election Commission Reports 1981–90.
*Statistically significant at .08 level.
[a]Statistically significant at .10 level.

members obtain more funds and outspend their senior colleagues, even at the same points in their House careers (tables 9 and 11)!

Finally, I have suggested that rent seeking reduces, or undermines, the effects of seniority by depreciating the value of the intrinsic returns to congressional service thereby increasing the incentives for rent seeking, even among senior members. Indeed, we observe increased rent-seeking behavior by senior incumbents although they still remain the lowest spenders and assemble the smallest campaign war chests. For these reasons, I have assumed that the differences in campaign expenditures and receipts across time and cohorts are a function of period and generation effects.

Analysis of campaign receipts. The major findings surrounding increases in campaign expenditures reappear in changes over time in campaign receipts (table 10). First, recent generations raise more campaign funds than older cohorts. For instance, those elected before 1968 raise considerably less campaign funds than those elected after 1976. Second, with the exception of the 1982 cohort, all cohorts exhibit significant longitudinal increases in their campaign receipts (table 10) during the ten-year period. Finally, more recent generations raise more campaign money than older cohorts at the same point in their House careers (table 11). In fact, the time-lag differences in campaign receipts (table 11) are even larger than those observed in campaign expenditures (table 9). In sum, there appear to be cross-sectional, longitudinal, and time-lag differences underlying the growth in campaign revenue. Once again, I have eliminated the possibility that seniority effects are present: the campaign receipts of senior House incumbents increase rather than decrease over the ten-year period, in sharp contrast to the hypothesized effect of se-

TABLE 10.   Mean Level of Campaign Receipts by Congressional Cohorts, 1981–90, in 1982 Dollars

Election Period	1966 or Before	1968–72	1974	1976	1978	1980	1982
1981–82**	203,816	271,239	234,102	184,872	235,578	437,645	
1983–84**	219,050	303,315	276,704*	236,802*	291,000*	297,809	333,885
1985–86	269,143*	367,332*	298,579a	252,847a	314,713a	304,647	324,309
1987–88	257,107a	345,943a	358,941*	279,329a	341,186a	339,979a	325,375
1989–90	250,093a	331,635a	354,983a	292,572a	358,392a	317,292	321,653
N	37	32	29	29	33	40	65

Source: Federal Election Commission Reports 1981–90.
*Statistically significant at .05 level: longitudinal difference (one-tailed test).
**Statistically significant at .05 level: cross-sectional difference.
aSignificant longitudinal difference between this mean and nonadjacent mean for this cohort.

TABLE 11. Time-lag Differences in Campaign Receipts among Cohorts, in 1982 Dollars

Years Served	1982	1980	1978	1976
2	333,885	437,645		
4**	324,309	297,809	235,578	
6*	325,375	304,647	291,000	184,872
8[a]	321,653	339,979	314,713	236,802
N	65	40	33	29

Source: Federal Election Commission Reports 1981–90.
*Statistically significant at .01 level.
**Statistically significant at .05 level.
[a]Statistically significant at .08 level.

niority in constraining rent seeking. Thus, campaign expenditures and receipts exhibit both period and cohort effects. Recent generations display a greater inclination to raise and spend large sums of money in the pursuit of congressional office than do older cohorts, and most congressional cohorts increased their campaign receipts and expenditures during the 1980s.

Of course, these data are not perfectly behaved. For example, there are several departures from monotonicity: those elected between 1968 and 1972 spend and raise more campaign funds than some of the cohorts entering Congress after that period, and some generations exhibit sporadic declines in raising and spending campaign funds over time. Despite these anomalies, there is evidence that generations differ in the raising and spending of campaign funds and that these differences persist over time.[5] In addition, significant increases over time in receipts and expenditures are evident within all but the most recent generation of incumbents. In conclusion, rent-seeking behavior within Congress seems to have risen during the 1980s as new generations raised levels of campaign spending and revenue and the rent-seeking milieu reduced whatever influence growing seniority might have in constraining rent seeking within the legislature.

Summary

There are two basic conclusions that can be drawn from the analyses presented in this chapter. First, the organization of Congress functions

---

5. If we restrict the comparison of changes in campaign expenditures and receipts over time to changes between presidential (or midterm) elections, the conclusions remain intact. Evidence for this contention also can be found in tables 8 and 10.

to enhance the financial returns that incumbent legislators can obtain from serving group interests. Since there are numerous institutional obstacles or legislative hurdles to the passage of legislation and even regulations, there is a substantial demand for legislator assistance, and many legislators stand to earn handsome financial returns for rendering assistance. Further, the institutional structure reduces the costs of supplying group services for legislators in possession of institutional power; this earns them more business. In addition, the absence of institutional mechanisms for assuring contractual performance on the part of legislators necessitates that price premiums are paid over and above the actual price of the service—a sort of protection money to assure that legislators do not renege on their promises to special interests. The second conclusion is that rent-seeking behavior, at least in terms of the raising and spending of campaign funds, has increased over time in response to both period and generational influences—that is, the rent-seeking milieu within Congress and society and the entrance of legislators who raise large sums of money and spend it lavishly on their reelection campaigns. Recent generations of House incumbents engage in these activities to a greater degree than older members, but all generations increased their rent-seeking activities during the 1980s.

I have now examined three of the four adverse selection hypotheses, and all receive empirical support. Rent-seeking legislators have exploited institutional arrangements for financial gain, as in the House bank scandal; rent seeking reduces the intrinsic returns to legislative service so that career politicians do not find congressional service alluring; and generational changes in the composition of Congress have resulted in increased rent-seeking behavior, such as increases in the raising and spending of campaign funds. In the next chapter, I examine the final hypothesis: rent seeking promotes the exit of career politicians—the retirement problem.

CHAPTER 6

The Retirement Problem

The adverse selection argument implies that there is a retirement, as well as a recruitment, problem: the exiting of those who prefer the intrinsic returns to legislative service—namely, career legislators. Evidence of the severity of the retirement problem can be seen in figure 14 where the trend in the seniority of House retirees (mean years of service) between 1790 and 1990 is illustrated. The figure reveals a clear and dramatic rise in the seniority of retirees around 1950, with the peak level of retiree seniority occurring in 1988 when the mean rises to 22.4 years of service.

Perhaps the growth in the exit of senior legislators is really nothing to worry about? It could be argued persuasively that the increased seniority of retirees is a natural by-product of the growth in congressional careerism. Congress has long been considered as incorporating established patterns of career advancement and developing norms and procedures that encourage members to devote a considerable proportion of their lives to congressional service (see Polsby 1968). Therefore, one reason why very senior members are departing may be simply because today's legislators are staying in office longer; hence, we might expect retiring legislators to be very senior. Table 12 presents a survival table, organized in ten-year congressional cohorts, describing the rate of survival for each cohort. Until the early 1900s, few legislators survived beyond the sixth term, but since the 1950s more than 20 percent of the entering cohorts remain in office beyond their tenth term. Clearly, career longevity can explain some of the unusual rise in the seniority of retirees. However, levels of attrition only tell part of the story.

In table 13 I report the reasons underlying departures. One important feature of this table is the increased number of House retirees who have left Congress (specifically, the House of Representatives) to pursue another office, either elected or appointed. For example, the percentage of House incumbents leaving to run for another office has risen since the 1930s. Senior members are not merely leaving the House to go into personal retirement: many pursue careers in the private sector, return to a prior vocation, or seek another public office. In fact, only

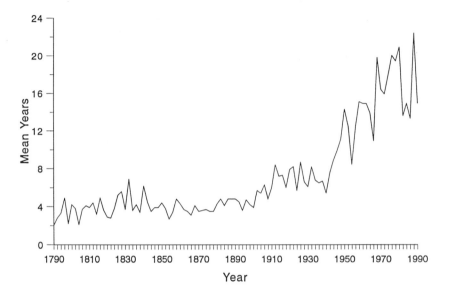

Fig. 14. Mean years of House service at retirement, 1790–1990. (Data from ICPSR Study No. 7803.)

ten percent of those retiring from the House of Representatives between 1789 and 1990 actually retired. The vast majority of retirees find other forms of employment once they leave Congress. In short, many senior legislators are leaving the House for more personally attractive opportunities. If Congress were ever viewed as a career unto itself, that

TABLE 12.   Attrition Within Congressional Cohorts, 1790–1979

Terms	1790–99	1800–1809	1810–19	1820–29	1830–39	1840–49	1850–59	1860–69	1870–79
2	55.9	61.6	46.2	55.9	58.2	45.9	46.2	48.9	52.5
3	33.5	37.3	21.3	31.4	20.2	17.6	16.3	24.0	25.6
4	20.2	19.8	12.1	17.7	9.0	8.1	8.0	10.9	14.3
5	14.9	13.3	8.2	9.8	4.7	5.0	4.6	5.7	9.0
6	12.2	8.7	5.1	5.5	2.4	2.6	2.9	2.9	5.3
7	9.0	5.3	2.9	3.1	1.1	1.4	2.0	1.8	3.4
8	7.4	3.0	1.9	1.9		.9	1.1	1.2	2.5
9	4.8	1.1	1.7	.5	.9	.5	.8	1.0	2.0
10+	2.1	.8	1.5	.5	.2	.2	.5	.8	1.5
N	188	263	413	417	534	579	612	487	712

Source: Roster of United States Congressional Officeholders and Biographical Characteristics of Members of the United States Congress, 1789–1991 (ICPSR 7803) 1991.

characterization may now be in serious need of review and perhaps revision.

Natural attrition within older congressional generations, therefore, may explain some of the increased tenure of House members at retirement, but the data describing the reasons for leaving the House suggest that legislators have exited the House to pursue other avenues of achievement and gratification rather than merely retiring from public life. Are legislators being lured away by the attraction of better-paying jobs? Probably some have left the House for this as well as other largely idiosyncratic reasons, but I believe that the decline in the value of a congressional career is at least partially responsible for the departure of career politicians in recent decades. This decline has been brought about by the same force that directly and indirectly reduces the attraction of legislative service for career politicians: increased rent seeking.

Explaining the Trend in the Exit of Senior Legislators

There is widespread recognition that congressional careers impose costs on legislators, but the diminution of the intrinsic returns to legislative service may be an underappreciated factor in congressional retirements. Political scientists generally agree that disaffection with service in Congress is a critical force in retirement decisions (Cooper and West 1981; Frantzich 1978; Hibbing 1982a). Several factors are often cited as promoting such dissatisfaction: growing workload, organizational hindrances (e.g., outdated institutional rules), constituent demands, and the need to raise campaign funds:

1880–89	1890–99	1900–1909	1910–19	1920–29	1930–39	1940–49	1950–59	1960–69	1970–79
61.1	58.4	68.0	70.8	68.7	70.4	65.6	81.5	81.2	86.5
30.1	33.1	49.6	52.4	58.8	54.3	53.2	72.6	72.1	76.8
18.0	24.4	36.1	41.0	46.5	44.3	44.6	62.2	65.1	65.1
10.6	18.7	27.4	32.8	36.9	34.5	37.9	52.9	53.3	54.5
7.1	15.7	20.1	26.5	27.5	26.5	33.8	44.0	47.2	46.7
6.0	11.6	15.1	22.7	19.5	21.6	29.7	37.5	39.3	41.9
4.3	8.6	10.8	17.4	15.9	16.7	25.3	30.8	33.2	38.2
2.8	7.2	8.5	12.8	11.2	13.1	20.8	25.5	26.5	36.5
1.5	4.7	7.5	8.8	9.4	11.1	17.3	20.6	21.9	35.6
604	722	482	603	447	551	465	333	328	351

Congress and the Rent-Seeking Society

TABLE 13. Reasons for Exiting the U.S. House by Ten-Year Cohorts, 1790–1989

Terms	1790–99	1800–1809	1810–19	1820–29	1830–39	1840–49	1850–59	1860–69	1870–79	1880–89
Lost election	10.0	14.4	19.9	32.5	30.7	25.1	30.9	27.2	31.6	31.9
Lost primary	1.1	.8	3.2	1.6	1.2	2.8	3.5	7.9	10.5	11.1
Died	21.1	10.6	7.7	11.1	8.5	10.8	5.3	7.2	7.0	8.1
Retired	35.6	43.9	49.8	44.0	48.3	54.1	51.0	51.5	46.9	41.5
Sought other office	1.1	1.5	1.4	1.2	1.8	2.2	1.1	1.0	1.0	3.5
Took federal office	10.0	3.8	3.2	2.1	2.7	1.9	.9	2.1	.5	1.5
Resigned	21.1	23.5	14.9	7.4	6.7	3.0	7.3	3.1	2.6	2.5
Appointed to Senate		1.5								
Still serving										
N	90	132	221	243	329	362	453	390	618	521

Source: Roster of United States Congressional Officeholders and Biographical Characteristiccs of Members of the United States Congress, 1789–1991 (ICPSR 7803) 1991.

As a result, the job of the congressman is far more onerous and unpleasant than it was a few decades ago. Members now lead very hectic and frenetic lives. The combination of their Washington and district duties results in long hours on the job and frequent travel. They thus have little time to spend with their families, and the pressures of the job also appear to cause more health problems at earlier ages than in the past. When in Washington, members are constantly confronted by the need to vote on numerous issues they know little about, frustrated by conflicts in committee meetings and overlaps in jurisdictions, and debilitated by the need to run continually from office to committee to floor and vice versa. They find practicing the basic politician's art of compromise more difficult and encounter considerable internal conflict between their desire to spend their time as legislators working on substantive policy questions that interest them and their perceived need to satisfy constituent requests, maintain a personal presence in their districts, and electioneer. (Cooper and West 1981, 289)

1890–99	1900–1909	1910–19	1920–29	1930–39	1940–49	1950–59	1960–69	1970–79	1980–89
32.7	31.6	36.1	37.8	34.1	37.4	37.3	32.0	19.7	13.3
13.7	12.3	13.2	15.1	15.6	13.3	7.5	6.7	4.0	1.7
9.5	15.4	15.9	15.7	15.1	10.1	8.4	5.5	4.6	1.0
38.0	31.8	24.8	20.7	24.0	25.4	31.6	26.5	14.8	3.0
2.3	3.7	·4.4	4.9	6.5	7.5	9.3	13.7	18.2	7.3
1.8	2.6	3.7	3.4	2.0	1.1	1.5	1.2	1.7	
1.9	2.6	1.9	2.5	2.7	4.5	1.8	2.1	3.7	.3
					.6	2.4	12.2	33.3	73.0
681	462	592	445	551	465	332	328	351	299

At least for career politicians, we could add the prominent role of rent seeking in Congress to this list of sources of dissatisfaction. From this perspective, the decline in intrinsic returns, brought about largely by increased rent-seeking demands, has hastened the departure of career politicians. This seems to be consistent with the findings from several studies (Cooper and West 1981; Hibbing 1982b; Moore and Hibbing 1992) that as members move up the seniority ladder, the inclination to retire rises rather than declines. For instance, Joseph Cooper and William West concluded:

> Thus, retirement has grown in the ranks of those members who ought to be the most resistant to it: among members who have made substantial personal commitments to and investments in House careers and who have attained important institutional rewards for their service. Moreover, this is true despite a sizable decline in the average age of House members. (1981, 292)

And seniority is related to retirements in both the House and the Senate, even when age is controlled (Hibbing 1982b; Livingston and Friedman

1993). This may seem a rather unexpected finding since senior members are in the best position to enjoy the benefits of legislative service and would seem to have little reason to retire (Hibbing 1982b).

The positive relationship between seniority and exits from the House has given rise to two contending views. Cooper and West have argued that "since increases in retirement have occurred among groups or categories of members who are advantaged rather than disadvantaged by the manner in which organizational rewards are distributed in the House, some negative alteration in the benefit-cost ratio of service must have taken place. If so, disaffection must have also increased as a concomitant effect" (1981, 293). Moore and Hibbing, in contrast, point out that the emergence of many of the difficulties cited as making service in the House less attractive were again present in the 1980s, but retirements declined:

> For the most part, all of the things that were alleged to have reduced job satisfaction in the 1970s (acerbic colleagues, byzantine committee structures, intrusive media, demanding constituents, incessant fund raising, and widespread disrespect for politicians) were present in the 1980s. If anything, public disrespect for members of Congress and the importance of fund raising have gone up, not down. Yet in the 1980s almost no one left Congress voluntarily. (1992, 825)

They offer an alternative to the disaffection hypothesis, arguing that successful reform and modification of the seniority system in the 1970s disadvantaged senior members, thereby prompting their retirement from the House. "No longer guaranteed either the powerful formal committee positions or the deference of their junior colleagues," Moore and Hibbing write, "their seniority became a liability rather than an asset, and many senior members departed voluntarily"[1] (1192, 826).

The Moore-Hibbing argument about the importance of changes in the seniority system in inducing exits is quite persuasive. However, at least one point in the argument is problematic: the trend in the exiting of career or senior House members appears to predate modifications in the seniority system that were introduced in the early 1970s. Specifically, the mean years of service of retirees rises to double digits in the late 1940s and early 1950s (fig. 14); hence, the exiting of career legislators was well

---

1. The reform of the seniority system no doubt reduced the intrinsic returns of a congressional career by eliminating the automatic acquisition of committee leadership positions by the most senior committee member.

underway before the 1970s. The retirement of senior legislators may have accelerated during the 1970s, but the retirement of senior legislators was not precipitated by changes in the seniority system since the exit of career legislators began decades earlier. There is, however, another explanation that is compatible with Moore and Hibbing's conclusion as well as the arguments of Cooper and West (1981): the exit of career legislators is a function of the decline in the intrinsic returns associated with careers in Congress. In the next several pages I will explore the significance of the above explanations for the exit of senior legislators: rent seeking, aging, declining institutional esteem, and the timing of seniority system reforms.

Statistical analysis. I suggested in chapter 2 that the intrinsic returns of congressional officeholding were related to the level of rent seeking in government and the popularity of Congress: intrinsic returns are diminished by high levels of unpopularity and rent-seeking behavior, resulting in the entrance of politicians who attach less value to the intrinsic returns of a congressional career. Legislators who have invested heavily in their congressional careers experience reduced intrinsic returns during periods of institutional unpopularity and high levels of rent seeking. While this is a problem for all politicians, it is particularly disconcerting to congressional careerists because of the sizable investments (sunk costs) they have incurred in their careers. If this is so, then high levels of popular dissatisfaction with Congress and rent seeking can accelerate the exit of career legislators. Senior legislators leave because they fear a loss in future intrinsic returns and perhaps a depreciation in the investments they have already made in their careers as congressional service becomes a focus of public ridicule.

I examine the possibility that the lengthening of the congressional career in past decades has created a natural tendency for legislators to retire with large amounts of seniority because they are staying in Congress for a longer period of time. If this is true, the age of retiring legislators should increase over time and such a pattern could produce the observed rise in the seniority of retirees. Therefore, I suspect that the rising seniority of House retirees is at least partially explained by the fact that members are extending their careers and retiring at later points in the life cycle. The Moore-Hibbing (1992) hypothesis—namely, that the institution of seniority reforms precipitated the observed departures of highly senior legislators—can also be tested by introducing a simple dummy variable that takes on the value of 1 with the institution of the reforms in 1975 and zero for all the years prior. The year 1975 was used to indicate the institution of reforms because it marks the ouster of three powerful committee chairmen—the first real threat to the role of seniority.

The relationships between the seniority of House retirees, institutional esteem, rent seeking, career aging, and the institution of seniority reforms can be described by the following functional relationship:

$$S = f(U, R, A, I),\tag{4}$$

where,

> S = mean years of House service at time of retirement,
> U = percentage of the electorate with unfavorable evaluations of congressional performance,
> R = pages in the *Federal Register,*
> A = mean age of House retirees,
> I = institution of reforms of seniority system.

Table 14 describes the results. The evidence suggests that there are two primary forces producing the retirement of very senior House members: the lengthening of the congressional career and the heightened levels of rent seeking in Congress. Both factors are statistically significant (table 14, eq. 1 and 2) and in the predicted directions. It is not too surprising that the growth in congressional careerism has resulted in retiring legislators accumulating long years of legislative service. Perhaps this is why so

TABLE 14. Rent Seeking, Congressional Unpopularity, and the Mean Years of Service of House Retirees, 1944–90

Variables	Equation 1		Equation 2	
	b	t-value	b	t-value
Number of pages of regulations (per 100 pages) (R)	.0085	2.335*	.0057	4.033**
Unpopularity of congressional performance (U)	.0578	.769	.0692	1.048
Mean age of House retirees (A)	.3547	2.394*	.3760	2.528*
Institution of congressional reforms in 1975 (I)	−2.7690	−.854		
Statistics:				
R^2		.67		.65
Adjusted R^2		.57		.58
Durbin-Watson		1.94		1.81
N		19		19

Source: Data compiled by author.
**p ≤ .01
*p ≤ .05

little significance has been attached previously to the increased seniority of House retirees. What is rather unexpected in light of past research on congressional retirements is the pronounced effect of the rent-seeking society. The growth in rent-seeking opportunities in Congress, as reflected in the rise in pages of federal regulations, detracts from legislative services at least for career politicians. As a result, senior legislators exit. This is a clear manifestation of the adverse effects of rent seeking on the composition of Congress.

If rent seeking is a major cause of congressional retirements, why has so little notice been given to this factor? Part of the reason rests in the fact that many studies of retirements have ignored this potential hypothesis. In some instances, researchers have relied heavily upon interviews with retirees, which are unlikely to reveal the significance of rent seeking in hastening exits. Since all legislators, whether or not they are initially motivated to do so, find it necessary to engage in rent-seeking activities during the course of their careers, prudence as well as fear of hypocrisy probably keep many retirees from singling out rent seeking.

Contrary to expectations, there is no statistical evidence that the unpopularity of Congress influences the retirement decisions of House members. There are a number of explanations for this null finding. First, senior legislators have a long period in which to establish their own "home styles" (Fenno 1978), and in doing so they may have succeeded, as many legislators do, in differentiating their own reputations from that of Congress in the minds of constituents. Hence, the reputations of these senior members may be more immune to fluctuations in congressional esteem and so institutional unpopularity weighs less heavily on their decisions to retire. Second, congressional unpopularity at earlier points in time might precipitate consideration of retirement, especially since retirement decisions are often made years in advance. Alternatively, perhaps the level of rent seeking is such a critical consideration in retirement decisions that it overwhelms other indications of declining intrinsic returns. In any event, I think it would be precipitous to discard the hypothesis that losses in institutional esteem encourage senior legislators to retire without more extensive study.

Clearly, rent-seeking behavior not only attracts noncareer politicians to congressional service (chap. 3); it also drives out career politicians! Admittedly, the evidence is fragile, but once again the relationships are robust and in the predicted directions. At the very least, this is further evidence that adverse selection may be more than mere intellectual folly—it represents a potential problem in the evolution of the U.S. Congress.

There is no doubt that the exit of senior legislators represents a problem that legislatures must cope with, but it also creates a positive externality by reducing the potential for dysfunctional last-period problems. As noted earlier, no matter how ethical individuals may be while in office, rational legislators have incentives to exploit their position for gain in their last term (Lott 1987; Lott and Reed 1989; Lott and Davis 1992; Zupan 1990). When politicians are no longer confronted with the need to stand for reelection and can no longer expect to enjoy the intrinsic returns of continued legislative service, we might expect expressions of opportunism to appear. Even career politicians who, by definition, value the intrinsic returns from public service have incentives to engage in opportunistic behavior in the last term of office. Is it rational to do otherwise? I believe so: career politicians are constrained from taking advantage of their position in the legislature prior to retirement because of the fear that *public disclosure* of their opportunistic behavior might damage their reputations and all they have invested in those reputations. This reduces the incentives for career politicians to engage in illegal, opportunistic, or unethical behavior in the last term of office. Ironically, then, adverse selection—despite its negative consequences—might actually impede the emergence of organizational problems in representational institutions, at least temporarily. If this is true, there should be no evidence of opportunistic rent-seeking behavior among recent congressional retirees. This proposition can be examined because of an explicit opportunity for legislators to increase their wealth through rent-seeking behavior in the last term: a provision in present election laws that allows some legislators—those elected before 1980—to keep any surplus campaign funds once they retire.

Rent-Seeking Behavior in the Last Period

If Congress has attracted recruits more interested in monetary reward than public service, we might expect organized attempts to *create* institutional arrangements (e.g., rules, laws) that can be exploited for financial gain. This is a reasonable explanation for why a complex legal loophole was planted in congressional amendments to the Federal Election Campaign Act (a measure packaged as legislative reform) that allows former members of Congress to pocket money they raised in their campaigns, provided the incumbent was sworn in before January 8, 1980, and left office before 1993. In short, retiring legislators elected before 1980 can leave office and retain all unused campaign funds for their own personal use! We might expect, therefore, that rent-seeking incumbents facing their *last election* would try to accumulate as large a campaign war chest as possible before retiring. Retiring congressional incumbents can maximize the amount of unused campaign funds simply by raising a considerable amount of campaign money—more than is necessary given electoral threats and past fund-raising efforts—and by spending as little as possible.

It is perhaps ironic that the loophole that allows members of Congress to leave office with their campaign war chests was part of a major legislative effort to reform the electoral and campaign process. One provision of the amendments to the 1971 Federal Election Campaign Act (passed in 1979) specified that campaign funds could *not* be converted by any person (any future member of Congress) for personal use, other than to defray necessary expenses incurred in connection with his or her duties as a holder of federal office, or to repay personal loans, the proceeds of which were used in connection with his or her campaign. Incumbents in the Ninety-sixth Congress, however, exempted themselves from this provision, requiring that it only apply to legislators taking office after January 8, 1980.

Eliminating this loophole became a rallying point for many legislative reformers, but their efforts failed to abolish the loophole outright. The "best" that could be accomplished was a provision in another congressional reform measure—Ethics Reform Act (1989)—that gradually phased out the grandfather clause that benefited incumbents elected before 1980. Grandfathered legislators were forced to decide whether to take their funds or remain in Congress without the right to do so after the convening of the One hundred and third Congress in January 1993. The rule also limited these legislators from taking an amount exceeding that which was on hand in their campaign accounts on the day the law was passed—November 30, 1989. Anything in excess of this amount could not be converted to personal use. Thus, incumbent members of Congress who were elected prior to 1980 can legally convert excess campaign funds to their own personal use providing they left office before 1993.

Even though many members have taken advantage of this loophole not all have converted these funds for *personal use*. Some have made charitable contributions or established scholarships at state universities, while others have contributed their leftover campaign funds to state and local party organizations.[2] Those who have decided to make personal use of their campaign war chests have done so in a variety of ways.

The easiest method for liquidating campaign war chests is done

---

2. For instance, Charles Whitley (D-N.C.) gave $40,000 to two small colleges in his district and Don Fuqua (D-Fla.) established a $100,000 endowment at the University of Florida.

simply by writing oneself a check for the remaining balance of funds, but some of the largest conversions of campaign funds have occurred as the result of an incumbent's death.[3] For example, Representative John Duncan (R-Tenn.) bequeathed $605,252 to his wife and family; Representative James Howard (D-N.J.) left $326,561 to his widow, and his colleague Bill Nichols (D-Ala.) bequeathed $438,561 to his heirs. Several legislators have also converted funds to cover legal costs resulting from charges of impropriety: Representatives Mario Biaggi (D-N.Y.), Robert Gracia (D-N.Y.), Jim Wright (D-Tex.), and Fernand St. Germain (D-R.I.). Another legal way of putting leftover campaign funds to personal use is to use residual funds as an expense account to cover postretirement office and career "transition" costs. These accounts are treated as personal expense accounts since almost any conceivable use of the money is allowed as long as some "political" purpose can be ascribed to the expenditure. This method also has the advantage of reducing the tax burden and media attention associated with directly converting campaign war chests to personal use.

While the instances in which incumbent legislators have converted campaign war chests to personal use may anger most citizens, many legislators have not done so. Instead, they have used their leftover funds to make charitable contributions to political, educational, and public-spirited entities. Irrespective of the final disposition of these leftover campaign funds—whether they serve altruistic or more personal ends—the question of opportunism among retirees remains: have House retirees exploited this loophole in the election laws in their last term of office? Such opportunism is what we might expect of rent-seeking politicians in their last period of officeholding, but not career legislators.

Data and analysis. For the purpose of this analysis I assume that legislators are wealth-maximizers who decide prior to each election whether it will be their last. They refrain from announcing the decision at that time because to do so would only hamper current efforts to raise voter support and campaign funds—rational groups would not contribute to a politician in the last period. If House incumbents seek to exploit their grandfathered advantage, they should increase the size of their campaign coffers by raising enormous sums of money while at the same time reducing their campaign expenditures in the last election period. Clearly, there is some risk involved in reducing campaign expenditures, but the risk may be worth it. After all, exiting with a large reserve of campaign funds might be construed as "fair" compensation

---

3. By simply writing himself a check for $345,000, Gene Taylor (R-Mo.) established the unflattering record for the highest amount taken by a living legislator.

for electoral defeat. This may explain why both Fernand St. Germain (D-R.I.) and Joseph Minish (D-N.J.) declined to spend more than $200,000 in available campaign funds to stave off subsequent electoral defeat.

To test this hypothesis I have compiled figures on the campaign receipts and expenditures of incumbents elected before 1980 who have retired between 1982 and 1990 (i.e., 56 representatives). Specifically, I expect opportunistic, rent-seeking retirees to raise more money in their final election period (last election before retirement) than in their previous two elections and to minimize their campaign expenditures in the final election period. To test this proposition I have conducted difference-of-means tests for paired samples. These t-tests are applied to the differences in the mean levels of receipts and expenditures between the final election period and earlier election periods. To be valid, the hypothesis requires that last-period receipts be significantly greater than campaign receipts in previous elections but that campaign expenditures show no appreciable increase in the last period. Why would a legislator intent upon maximizing excess campaign funds increase campaign spending beyond the level that safely returned him or her to office in the recent past? Such overinvestment only erodes the value of the "golden parachute" (excess campaign funds). These hypothesized relationships are specified in table 15.

Some legislators have defended the accumulation of large war chests as a necessity to combat future competition with "deep pockets" of their own. While the likelihood of such an event seems remote in light of the impoverished state of most congressional challengers, I examine this possibility by introducing controls for electoral safety into the analysis. I have taken an unusually broad definition of electoral safety—electoral support greater than 70 percent—to assure that the measurement of electoral

TABLE 15. Predicted Relationships between Campaign Receipts and Spending Prior to Retirement

Campaign Activity	Election Period Comparison		
	T: T − 1	T: T − 2	T − 1: T − 2
Spending	N.S.	N.S.	N.S.
Receipts	SIG.	SIG.	N.S.

Note: T = Last election period (two years) prior to retirment.
T − 1 = Penultimate election period.
T − 2 = Election period four years prior to last period.
N.S. = Statistical relationship is not significant at .01 level.
SIG. = Statistical relationship is significant at .01 level.

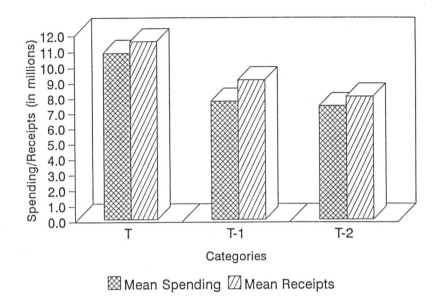

Fig. 15. Campaign spending and receipts. (Data compiled by author from Federal Election Commission Reports 1981–90.)

insecurity (< 70 percent) allows for ample overestimation by incumbents. This determination of electoral safety is also necessitated by the fact that few incumbents in the study received less than 60 percent of the vote in any election.

Figure 15 describes the relationship over time between campaign receipts and expenditures during the three election periods specified in table 15 (T, T − 1, T − 2). On the vertical axis is the number of dollars received and spent. The horizontal axis is divided into the three election periods—prior to retirement (T), penultimate election period (T − 1), and the election period four years prior to the last election period (T − 2). The changes in campaign expenditures and receipts over the six-year period mirror the comparative statics in the statistical analysis: there does not appear to be a last-period problem.

Specifically, there seems to be little evidence of opportunism in the raising and spending of campaign funds. While House members do indeed raise more money in the final election period than in the penultimate campaign, election expenses also increase in the last campaign (fig. 15). Such a pattern is not what we would expect of legislators trying to

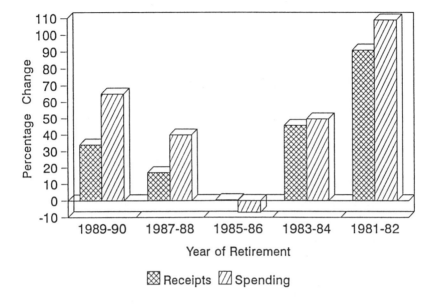

Fig. 16. Change in campaign spending. (Data compiled by author from Federal Election Commission Reports 1981–90.)

maximize their returns in their final election. When the data are disaggregated by retiring cohorts, it is clear that the pattern of increased spending, as well as fund-raising, in the final election campaign is *not* peculiar to specific retirement cohorts (fig. 16). With the exception of those retiring after the 1984 election (1985–86 cohort), campaign spending increased at even a greater rate than campaign receipts in the last election. Table 16 reports the significance of the differences (in means) between the final three elections. Again, the findings illustrated in figures 15 and 16 reappear: there have been significant changes in both campaign receipts *and* spending between the final and penultimate election campaigns.

It might be argued that increased spending should be construed as characteristic of rent-seeking behavior in the last period: legislators draw down their campaign war chests (to avoid public outrage) through lavish and frivolous expenditures during the course of their last campaign thereby avoiding the thorny question of what to do with campaign surpluses. For example, there is evidence that some incumbents "with easy access to money from special interests turned their campaign treasuries

TABLE 16.   Mean Levels of Campaign Spending and Receipts Compared over Three Elections Periods, in Dollars

Election Period Comparisons	Campaign Activity			
	Receipts	t-value	Spending	t-value
1. T: T − 1	Significant*	2.54	Significant*	2.39
T	225,722.32		208,445.46	
T − 1	184,152.25		159,222.11	
2. T: T − 2	Significant*	2.81	Significant[a]	2.18
T	225,722.32		208,445.46	
T − 2	165,892.13		152,760.00	
3. T − 1: T − 2	Nonsignificant	1.12	Nonsignificant	.33
T − 1	184,152.25		159,222.11	
T − 2	165,892.13		152,760.00	

Source: Federal Election Commission Reports 1981–90.
*Significant at .01 level.
[a]Significant at .017 level.

into slush funds to pay for personal items such as vacations and country club dues" (*Washington Post* 1992, 34). Other legislators have used excess campaign funds to purchase office buildings or have paid lavish sums to political consultants.[4] Therefore, increased campaign spending in the last election might indeed signify opportunistic behavior.

It is, of course, extremely difficulty to differentiate objectively between what is necessary to a successful campaign and what is frivolous. However, increased spending on the part of electorally safe legislators in their last election campaign could be construed as unnecessary expenditures. Electorally safe members of Congress have no reason to increase their campaign spending in their last election campaign except to exhaust the funds remaining in their war chests. Even such arguable evidence of opportunistic behavior is missing: electorally safe incumbents

---

4. While personal use of campaign funds is illegal under both federal laws and congressional rules, the Senate allows its members to use campaign funds to support officially connected activities while House incumbents are allowed to use the money for most political expenses. These definitions are so broad that over the years few expenditures have been questioned and challenged. Dan Rostenkowski's (D-Ill.) use of excess campaign funds is illustrative of the types of personal benefits that can be supported by these funds. "For example, nearly a third of the $358,331 in operating expenses reported by Rostenkowski's campaign and his PAC in 1990 and 1991 went for items that enhanced his lifestyle or income—travel, chauffeurs, car insurance, cable TV bills, dinner out, a golf caddy, and rental payments to himself and his family" (*Congressional Quarterly Weekly Report,* June 5, 1993, 1403). Equally outrageous was his use of campaign funds to hire "golf consultants"— four golf pros hired to give pointers to and play with his friends and supporters at an annual country club outing he hosts each year near his summer home in Wisconsin!

TABLE 17. The Impact of Electoral Safety on Campaign Spending and Receipts over Three Election Periods, in Dollars

Election Period Comparisons	Penultimate Election > 70%		Penultimate Election < 70%	
	Spending	Receipts	Spending	Receipts
1. T: T − 1	Nonsignificant	Nonsignificant	Significant*	Significant*
T	164,098.97	193,000.19	263,435.12	266,297.76
T − 1	149,982.10	169,959.58	170,679.72	201,751.16
t-value	.54	1.00	2.82	2.85
2. T: T − 2	Nonsignificant	Nonsignificant	Significant*	Significant*
T	164,098.97	193,000.19	263,435.12	266,297.76
T − 2	145,466.74	166,352.61	161,803.64	165,321.12
t-value	.47	.80	3.67	4.62
3. T − 1: T − 2	Nonsignificant	Nonsignificant	Nonsignificant	Nonsignificant
T − 1	149,982.10	169,959.58	170,679.72	201,751.16
T − 2	145,466.74	166,352.61	161,803.64	165,321.12
t-value	.15	.14	.36	2.09

Source: Federal Election Commission Reports 1981–90.
*Significant at .01 level.

exhibit *no* significant increase in either the raising or spending of campaign funds in their last election (table 17). Only those who received less than 70 percent of the popular vote in their penultimate election exhibit increases in *both* spending and receipts. In short, the lack of high levels of electoral safety, rather than greed, seems to underlie increases in the raising and spending of campaign funds by retiring legislators.

Why was such an obvious opportunity to increase one's wealth ignored by so many rational legislators? One explanation for the apparent lack of a last-period problem in campaign financing is that politicians do not know when they are in the last period. Hence, they are ill prepared to strategically manipulate the campaign finance process. This is, of course, an alternative to one of the assumptions that guides the analysis. I know of no way to refute or validate either of these assumptions empirically nor am I aware of any unobtrusive evidence that might serve this purpose. Hence, I cannot discount the possibility that the observed pattern in campaign spending activity is a function of the inability of legislators to recognize that they are in the last period. I would only point out that *if* politicians behave strategically, as many characterizations suggest (Downs 1957; Kalt and Zupan 1984), it is not beyond reason to expect them to anticipate their last election.[5] (Moreover, if

5. For instance, Stephen Frantzich (1978, 257) found that at least 50 percent of the House retirees interviewed in 1974 had decided prior to their last election (1972) to retire,

politicians are unaware of when they are in the last period, a last-period problem could not exist ipso facto.)

I favor a different explanation: there does not appear to be a significant increase in rent-seeking behavior in the last period because senior legislators have incentives to maintain their brand-name capital (reputation) because it is salvageable.[6] Hence, career legislators have incentives to protect their investments that might be severely damaged by the legal, but ethically questionable, practice of retaining excess campaign funds. In short, retirement from politics is no signal that one is at the end of the earning stream. Hence, career politicians do not confront last-period situations.[7]

Summary

In this chapter, I examined two related aspects of the retirement problem—the exit of career legislators. On the one hand, the loss of career legislators is an important indicator of the diminished value of the intrinsic returns from a congressional career. On the other hand, the retirement of career politicians reduces the potential for last-period problems.

The increased retirement of senior legislators is not only a reaction to the growth in congressional careerism. Admittedly, most legislators now establish long careers in Congress—providing their constituents go along. Hence, we expect retiring legislators to have accumulated long

---

but none of them announced their intentions until after the elections, and two-thirds waited until the second year of their term to formally announce their decisions.

6. Trustworthy legislators (or politicians) may receive a lucrative job or a ceremonial post in some corporation upon leaving office (see, for instance, Eckert 1981). Moreover, one's children and relatives may play upon the good reputation of a former politician to gain political office. Furthermore, if a legislator acts opportunistically when it is rational to do so, those who do business with him or her (for example, employment after retirement) will need to take precautions to assure that he or she does not continue the habit. This raises the costs of doing business with rent-seeking legislators (monitoring and policing costs increase) and undoubtedly reduces returns as business gravitates to less costly—more trustworthy—legislators. When future returns are less than those earned through opportunistic behavior rational politicians shirk. The findings presented in this analysis suggest, however, that career politicians expect to earn handsome ex post facto returns from their dutiful years in the House of Representatives.

7. Klein, Crawford, and Alchian make a similar point: "the potential loss of value of indefinitely long-lived salable brand-name assets can serve as deterrents to cheating even where the contract between two parties has a last period. If one party's reputation for nonopportunistic dealings can be sold and used in later transactions in an infinite-time-horizon economy, the firm that cheats in the 'last period' to any one buyer from the firm experiences a capital loss" (1978, 304).

years of congressional service. Nonetheless, a large number of legislators leave voluntarily after long years of service to pursue other opportunities rather than having to be carried from Congress in the throes of death. Quite frequently, senior legislators do not "retire" in the normal sense of the word but return to prior vocations, establish new careers, or find attractive self-employment. What, then, has made retirement from Congress more attractive to career legislators?

Two factors seem to account for a large amount of the variation in the exits of senior legislators over time: levels of rent-seeking behavior and the lengthening of congressional careers. I have demonstrated that the mean years of service of retirees in the House rises in response to increases in pages of federal regulations (rent-seeking opportunities) and to the aging of House retirees. These two variables account for over 60 percent of the variation in the mean number of years of House retirees. The retirement hypothesis, therefore, is supported.

Even if the intrinsic returns of a legislative career could reduce rent seeking among members of Congress, legislators in their last term of office might easily forsake these returns for more material rewards. Without the expectation of future intrinsic returns, exiting career legislators might be expected to indulge their base instincts and desires. I examined this possibility by analyzing the raising and spending of campaign funds by retiring legislators who were permitted by law to retain all campaign surpluses for private use upon their retirement from Congress. Rent-seeking legislators might be expected to increase campaign fund-raising efforts and reduce campaign expenditures in their last election in an effort to increase the surplus they can pocket. Career politicians can be expected to refrain from such opportunistic behavior. I found no evidence of such a contrivance. I have argued that the value of one's reputation, especially its relevance for post-elective-office opportunities, constrains career politicians from engaging in opportunistic behavior.[8] Politicians with sterling reputations after years of public service stand to gain financially upon retirement. As long as retirees value their reputations because of the investments they have made, and the returns they expect to obtain, last-period problems should not appear with any regularity. But if the patterns in the entrance of amateurs and the departure of career politicians continue, it is inevitable that legislators without

---

8. If reputations constrain last-period problems, why don't they also constrain rent seeking in Congress? They probably do constrain rent seeking, but the influx of noncareer politicians (chapter 3) reduces the effectiveness of reputational capital in limiting such behavior. Rent seeking might be even more extensive if it were not for the effects of reputations!

large career investments will fill the ranks of congressional retirees. If so, the potential for last-period problems will increase.

Why did concern over one's reputation reduce the occurrence of last-period problems in the raising and spending of campaign funds but could not constrain abuses at the House bank? We should not underestimate the visibility of unethical practices in curbing opportunistic behavior. The House bank was largely a private organization that prided itself on confidentiality while the provision in the election laws that permitted some legislators to keep excess campaign funds gained wide notoriety. In the former instance, unethical behavior was less risky since there was little probability of a legislator's financial dealings with the House bank becoming public, short of a full-blown congressional investigation! In the latter instance, legislators knew from the start that the disposition of campaign surpluses would receive considerable media attention and inquiry. As the risks of publicity increase so does the effectiveness of reputations in constraining unethical behavior.

It should be clear from the analysis and findings in the previous chapters that the intrinsic returns from legislative service are ineffective in curbing rent seeking. The ineffectiveness of seniority in establishing an equilibrium to the rent-seeking activities of legislators (raising and spending campaign funds) necessitates an examination of other mechanisms for controlling that behavior. In the next chapter, I describe and assess the value of various mechanisms designed to constrain the capacity of legislators to reap financial gain from congressional service.

CHAPTER 7

Controlling Legislators

Economists Joseph Kalt and Mark Zupan (1984, 283) identify five attributes of the market for legislative seats that reduce the ability of citizens to control their elected officials: (1) voters confront all-or-nothing choices in selecting policymakers offering large bundles of "goods" (issues); (2) voters have poor incentives to become well informed about their representative's behavior; (3) constituent-owners have few incentives to organize because of attenuated property rights; (4) imperfect competition exists in the political market; and (5) there exist conditions conducive to opportunism. The implication is that legislator-agents are imperfectly policed by their principals—voters. In conjunction with the characteristics of the legislative process, the imperfect monitoring of legislators assures that those who prefer material to intrinsic gain can benefit through rent-seeking activities. As the analysis in chapter 5 revealed, increased tenure neither reduces rent-seeking activity nor even constrains its growth. Moreover, those who are probably restrained the most because of the size of their (sunk) investments and their preferences for intrinsic returns—career legislators—are exiting. Clearly, rent seeking is an important problem for the operation of Congress since we have no assurance that it can be effectively constrained by longevity in Congress or the diminishing marginal productivity of rent seeking. If new entrants seize opportunities for financial gain and those who remain fail to reduce their rent-seeking behavior, Congress will struggle with persistently low levels of public esteem and an increased probability of scandals. This is, of course, the most pessimistic outcome that might be expected.

A more encouraging note might be sounded because of the existence of several mechanisms that could conceivably constrain rent seeking: reputational capital, attractiveness of the office, loss of pension or other type of "performance" bond (Becker and Stigler 1974),[1] postelective em-

---

1. "Enforcers post a bond equal to the temptation of malfeasance, receive the income on the bond as long as they are employed, and have the bond returned if they behave themselves until retirement" (Becker and Stigler 1974, 602).

ployment, monitoring, future employment through the auspices of the political parties (Barro 1973), and elections. Some of these mechanisms of control have received little attention (e.g., postelective employment) while others appear to receive too much emphasis (e.g., elections). Nonetheless, all are capable of constraining rent seeking to some degree. In this chapter I describe how some mechanisms constrain rent-seeking behavior in Congress.

Reputational Capital

Most approaches to the effects of reputations consider them as serving two functions: low-cost signals of the future voting habits of politicians for voters who have few incentives to gather any information about the candidates (Downs 1957) and binding "a representative to certain positions from which he might otherwise be induced to deviate during his term of office" (Dougan and Munger 1989, 121). The latter purpose is particularly important from the perspective of this study: since "slack" exists in the legislative process (e.g., lack of monitoring), legislators may engage in "shirking" by reneging on their promises to voters in response to pressures or enticements from interest groups. Ideological reputations reduce the likelihood of reneging because they reflect investments of "capital" that will be sacrificed in casting votes inconsistent with that ideological identity. Hence, ideological reputations function as a bond to assure faithful performance in office.

A reputation as an honest legislator serves the same purposes as an ideological reputation: it reduces the likelihood of opportunistic behavior. A reputation for honesty can also be validated in the same manner as ideological reputations: by taking actions consistent with one's reputation. The ideologue casts ideological votes in Congress and emphasizes ideological themes in his or her reelection campaigns. Honest legislators refrain from engaging in unethical practices in Washington, and they point with pride to the absence of their names on lists of abusers at the House restaurant, post office, and bank, for example. In short, each time there is an exposé of congressional misconduct, legislators who are not involved in the scandal can use that fact to validate their claim to being an honest politician. And honesty pays off at election time. Honesty is one of the characteristics most frequently mentioned by voters in evaluating legislators and a major reason why voters trust their representative (Parker 1989a).

Ideological reputations do not preclude the establishment of reputations for honesty, and both serve to bind legislators to their promises. However, there is no reason to believe that ideological reputations can in any way constrain rent-seeking or wealth-maximizing behavior on the part of legislators (see chapter 3). This is why a reputation for honesty may be more important than an ideological reputation in constraining rent-seeking behavior. There is no ideological tenor to the rent-seeking activities of legislators (liberals and conservatives alike engage in rent seeking) that might make such activities repulsive, but for the politician making investments in his or her reputation for honesty such activities are an anathema. Reputational capital works something like this: politicians make investments in their own reputations ("brand names") that earn them a reasonable return if they remain honest; dishonesty depreciates one's reputation, thereby destroying a politician's investment capital. This capital serves to enhance a legislator's standing with his or her constituents, assuring future electoral safety, and freedom to maneuver— discretion—in Washington.

If honesty pays and dishonesty costs, there should be evidence that honest legislators earn more than dishonest ones. It is difficult, if not impossible, to obtain information on the earnings of former legislators. This renders a direct test of the premise that a reputation for honesty earns legislators handsome ex ante returns highly unlikely. Since information on the value of postelective employment is lacking, it is necessary to find some substitute that might serve as a proxy. The best information on the employment opportunities of congressional retirees that I could obtain was gleaned from biographical sources. I compiled information on the number of positions of employment held during the five years after their retirement by House members leaving Congress between 1967 and 1985. In determining the number of job opportunities, I examined a variety of biographical sources. I was able to obtain complete (five-year) information on 162 former legislators who sought employment upon their departure from the House. The hypothesis is that involvement in a scandal costs a legislator dearly when he or she is seeking postelective employment—it limits his or her job opportunities. The dependent variable is the number of positions of employment held by former House members during the five years after their retirement from Congress. A word of caution: this is a necessarily crude analysis of the employment opportunities available to exiting legislators, but it is the best that can be obtained with the information currently available. In addition to a dummy variable indicating whether or not the retiree was involved in a congressional scandal, variables are included to represent the impact of party, age, and leadership position on the earning opportunities of former

House members.[2] These relationships, specified in the following manner, are subjected to OLS regression:

$$E = f(S, A, L, P), \tag{5}$$

where

E = number of positions of employment held five years after retiring from the House of Representatives,

S = involvement in a congressional scandal; coded 1 if legislator was involved in a scandal and zero otherwise,

A = age of retiree at time of retirement,

L = position in legislature, coded 3 if retiree served as a party or committee leader, 2 if retiree was a subcommittee leader, and 1 if the retiree held no position of leadership,

P = party of retiree, coded 1 if retiree was a Democrat and 2 if retiree was a Republican.

The hypothesis regarding the effects of scandals on earning opportunities is that since involvement in a scandal makes a legislator a poor contractual risk (susceptible to shirking), those censured or convicted of wrongdoing will have fewer offers of gainful employment. Older retirees might be expected to have greater job opportunities because they have had a longer time to cultivate the contacts that are so advantageous to postelective employment. Similarly, legislative leaders can be expected to have a greater number of job-earning opportunities than less powerful members because their positions enable them to ingratiate themselves with special interests. Finally, the close association of the Republican Party with the interests of business suggests that Republicans should have a greater number of job opportunities than Democrats.

The findings are presented in table 18. There is no evidence that age at retirement or a position of legislative leadership influences the number of job opportunities enjoyed by House retirees. Party, however, does influence these opportunities in the expected fashion: House Republicans enjoyed an edge in postelective employment over their Democratic counterparts. While not highly significantly (alpha $\leq$ .08), involvement in congressional scandals does reduce the job opportunities available to

---

2. The list of House members involved in congressional scandals was obtained from the Committee on Standards of Official Conduct, U.S. House of Representatives, April 1992 (Committee on Standards, 1992). Only legislators that the committee found guilty of violating ethics rules or legislative statutes are considered to have been involved in a scandal.

TABLE 18. Predicting the Number of Job Opportunities of House Retirees

Variables	b	Standard Error	t-value	Significance
Involvement in a scandal (S)	−.616	.352	−1.750	.08
Age of retiree (A)	−.005	.006	−.922	.36
Leadership position (L)	.057	.117	.485	.63
Political party (P)	.538	.212	2.543	.01
Constant	1.302	.513	2.540	.01
Statistics:				
R^2 .07				
N 162				

Source: Data compiled by author.

House retirees. These results must be viewed as both tentative and exploratory given the fragile nature of the data, but the findings are consistent with the premise that a reputation for dishonesty costs a legislator in terms of the postelective opportunities available upon retirement. However, the effects of involvement in a scandal seem rather modest: scandalized legislators can expect to receive about one less employment opportunity in the ten years following their retirement from the House ($b = -.616$).

I suspect that the effects of dishonesty are far more costly than I have uncovered since the analysis neglects the issues of compensation and the quality of the job opportunities facing honest and scandalized legislators.[3] Respected politicians gain access to opportunities often denied the disreputable, such as partnerships in prestigious law firms or endowed professorships at major universities. Hence, there are more markets for the highly respected in which to sell one's services. This should increase their postelective earnings. Perhaps more importantly, less respected politicians are poor contractual risks because of their penchant for opportunism. Only industries that benefited from the actions of a disreputable (or opportunistic) public official are likely to provide him or her with postelective office opportunities, but even these industries will be forced to pay price premiums (Klein and Leffler 1981) and/or incur monitoring costs (Alchian and Demsetz 1972) to assure performance. If so, such industries will incorporate these costs into the

---

3. This is, perhaps, the most relevant issue: the quality of the jobs held by respected and scandalized legislators after leaving Congress. Since it is impossible to classify employment opportunities as high- or low-quality jobs because of the sparse information about the nature of the jobs held by former legislators, I can only speculate that the quality of the job opportunities (e.g., esteem, visibility, importance) confronting scandalized legislators is considerably "lower" than that facing respected politicians. This seems a valuable question for future research.

compensation paid opportunistic politicians thereby reducing their earnings compared to those of more trustworthy politicians. Nonetheless, a pronounced advantage for honest politicians in postelective employment is not evident.

The importance of brand names (reputations) in reducing opportunistic behavior has received little attention because they are often viewed as representing nonsalvageable capital (investments) that are ineffective in deterring opportunistic behavior in the last period of officeholding. In the market, the value of brand names rests in inducing future sales; in politics, elected officials refrain from opportunism because of the fear of losing the next election and foregoing the future returns that go along with officeholding. If politicians are in their final period of office, however, no future returns are foregone, and the value of a respected brand name disappears.

> politicians could make sunk investments (e.g., political brand name) that they earn some competitive return on in each subsequent period. If the present value of this premium is greater than the gain to cheating, the politician will not cheat. . . . However, sunk investments cannot eliminate opportunistic behavior in the last period when a politician has decided to retire and thus knows with certainty that he will no longer face re-election. (Lott 1987, 170)

While this argument makes considerable sense, it ignores the possibility that one's reputation affects postelective earnings.

Increasing the Returns to Legislative Service

If the legal returns to congressional service are sufficiently attractive, rational politicians have strong incentives to avoid unethical or illegal activities that might incite a voter revolt at the next election. As I have noted, the returns to congressional service encompass both intrinsic and material rewards. Hence, increasing the material and/or the intrinsic returns from congressional service should encourage rational legislators to ignore the extralegal financial opportunities associated with congressional office. With respect to the material benefits of officeholding, economist Robert Barro suggests that salary might be "viewed as an instrument which . . . can be utilized to effect a certain rate of substitution between private and public goods" (1973, 36). Simply put, a higher explicit salary for legislators would reduce the attractiveness of the implicit income-earning opportunities associated with legislative service because of the expected loss in income likely to result if such unethical activities were revealed to voters.

Barro makes a good argument, sustained with formidable mathematical derivations, but I remain skeptical because there is no evidence that increasing the salaries of House incumbents has even enhanced the attractiveness of a congressional career! For instance, there is no significant relationship between terms of service in the House of Representatives (between 1881 and 1988) and congressional salaries (Parker 1992a, 78–79). If the explicit or legal salary associated with congressional office is insufficient in encouraging long careers in Congress, it will probably also be inadequate in curbing avarice within the legislature. Moreover, increases in salary have historically received little public support, and such increases might, in fact, actually induce even greater suspicion of the motives of those in public service. A more effective way to increase the returns to legislative service would be to enhance the intrinsic rewards of a congressional career, perhaps by strengthening the seniority system.

From the perspective of this inquiry, one of the simplest and most effective means of enhancing intrinsic returns can be found in the role played by seniority within the institution. This contention runs counter to most scholarly opinion about the value of the seniority system to the legislative process. I dissent from this position because I feel too little attention has been given to the significance of the intrinsic returns to congressional service. In a real sense, reforms of the seniority system have had some negative consequences or external costs—namely, a reduction in the intrinsic returns associated with career longevity.

The seniority rule has been attacked on numerous grounds. Critics contend that by rewarding age and long service the seniority system builds a generation gap into legislative decision making thereby giving greater power to those least attuned to the contemporary needs of society.[4] The system has also been assailed for overrepresenting one-party areas of the nation, namely rural and conservative interests, at the expense of other regions. And the seniority system has no positive benefits in terms of "responsible" political parties. It obstructs party cohesion by creating independent centers—a cadre of committee chairs independent

---

4. The seniority system is a mechanism for selecting the leaders of congressional committees. It entails the ranking of legislators in each party according to their years of consecutive service on a committee. The seniority system provides a route of succession to committee leadership positions: the senior member of the majority party becomes the committee chair and the senior member from the minority party assumes the position of the ranking minority member on the committee. Subcommittee leadership positions are allocated in an identical fashion.

of their party's leaders because the latter have no control over their selection—and reinforces antiparty tendencies by favoring the appointment of legislators from safe districts who are most likely to be out of step with current party positions.

In defending the seniority rule, proponents emphasize the harmony that results, the emphasis that the system places on experience, and the lack of a more suitable alternative. For example, the seniority rule is deemed beneficial because it operates to diffuse hurt feelings on the part of those passed over for appointment—no matter the disappointment, they know that their turn will eventually come. This produces a more cooperative atmosphere both in Congress and in its individual committees. The seniority rule also assures that leaders are unusually familiar and experienced with the subject matter, budgets, and agency personnel associated with a committee's jurisdiction. Defenders also contend that the system, despite its flaws, is preferable to any alternative.

My objective in briefly describing some of the major arguments defending and attacking the seniority system is to point out that no consideration is given to the effects of the seniority "rule" in enhancing the intrinsic returns from congressional service. Neither the defenders nor the detractors of the seniority system consider the obvious positive consequences associated with the seniority rule: increased intrinsic returns from continuous legislative service. Clearly, the longer legislators are in Congress, the greater their appreciation of the seniority system. Thus, legislative efforts designed to weaken the force of seniority in congressional organization unconsciously diminish the intrinsic returns to legislative service.

Fortunately, the seniority system has withstood such assaults. In fact, the seniority system has been adhered to quite faithfully, even though it is mentioned nowhere in the formal rules of Congress and despite the adoption of procedures for *electing* committee leaders. In the twentieth century, the seniority rule has rarely been violated and then only in exceptional circumstances. For example, two southern Democrats were stripped of their committee seniority in the House because they had supported the Republican presidential candidate, Barry Goldwater, in 1964. Even requiring the election of committee leaders has done little to disrupt the seniority ladder to committee power. Although three House committee leaders were denied reappointment by a vote of the Democratic Caucus in 1975, this was a truly brief departure since the rule has been almost religiously followed in subsequent selections of committee leaders.

The force of the seniority rule is also evident in the practices used in selecting *subcommittee* leaders. Before 1973, House subcommittee chairs were appointed by the chair of the full committee, but the selection is now determined by a vote of the majority party members on the committee. Under this appointment system, committee seniority has been generally followed in selecting subcommittee leaders. "Application of the rule of committee seniority predicts which committee members will chair sub-committees in about 90 percent of the cases" (Wolanin 1974, 701). In some instances, committees emphasize subcommittee seniority in appointing subcommittee chairs (e.g., Appropriations), but most followed full-committee seniority in making these selections (Goldstone 1975). Adherence to the seniority norm did not dissipate after 1973 when sub-committee chairs were elected by the majority party members on the committee: most senior members who ranked high enough in seniority to warrant a subcommittee chair received one. In sum, despite changes in the method of selection, seniority continues to be a dominant criterion for choosing committee and subcommittee leaders.

The seniority system assures that a legislator's influence or power accrues with longevity in office, and increases in power make consumption of the intrinsic benefits of congressional service more rewarding. The seniority system, therefore, serves as an important constraint on unethical behavior associated with rent seeking, but it remains to be seen how such a rule might be expanded or enriched to further enhance the intrinsic returns from a congressional career.[5] It may be that we have done all we can to enhance the value of seniority.

It might be suggested that the intrinsic returns could be enhanced by boosting the esteem associated with legislative service. This seems rather improbable given the interests of legislators in attacking the institution (Fenno 1978; Parker 1992a) and those that lead it in their constituency visits. In addition, while all members gain from serving in a popular institution, there is a free-rider problem that dooms efforts to promote this collective good. Hence, restoring confidence in Congress—to the extent that the effort is dependent upon the willingness of legislators to contribute to that goal—is likely to experience limited success.

One of the objectives underlying efforts aimed at reforming Congress is to elevate (or restore) public esteem for the institution and its members. This serves to increase the intrinsic returns associated with a

---

5. One final point: longevity in office is often interpreted as a problem with consider-able negative externalities. Reforms have been formulated to remedy this problem, chief among them, term limitations. There are a number of problems with imposing term limitations, not the least of which is the institutionalization of last-period problems, and their impact remains unclear at best. Nonetheless, one implication is clear: term limitations would destroy the intrinsic returns associated with career longevity and therefore the capacity of such returns to constrain rent seeking.

congressional career (e.g., respect, admiration). Since restoring, or increasing, public esteem is a collective good—everyone reaps the benefit—no single legislator has sufficient incentives to provide the good or to contribute to its provision. Simply put, legislators can consume the good without paying in any way for its provision—they are classic free riders. Thus, Congress is generally unable to take action that would elevate public esteem for the institution because of the free-rider problem associated with collective efforts. Rational legislators would rather leave the efforts at restoring public confidence in Congress to others while still enjoying the fruits of the resulting effort, if it is at all successful.

Admittedly, legislative reforms designed to bolster public confidence occasionally gain congressional approval, but not without a struggle. When they do pass, it is usually the result of the efforts of a handful of legislators who place such a high value on the intrinsic returns of congressional service that they are willing to take it upon themselves to shepherd the reforms through Congress. That is, they are prepared to incur all the costs required in enacting legislative reforms. In such instances, we might expect a collective good to be provided:

> there are members who would be better off if the collective good were provided, even if they had to pay the entire cost of providing it themselves, than they would be if it were not provided. . . . [T]he greater the interest in the collective good of any single member, the greater the likelihood that member will get such a significant proportion of the total benefit from the collective good that he will gain from seeing that the good is provided, even if he has to pay all of the cost himself. (Olson 1965, 34)

David Mayhew has suggested a similar solution to the collective goods problem of inducing "at least some members to work toward keeping the institution in good repair" (1974, 146). Mayhew contends that prestige and power within Congress are accorded those engaged in institutionally protective activities:

> the most interesting paid protectors are those in official positions— elected leaders in both houses and members of the three "control committees" in the House [Rules, Ways and Means, Appropriations]. . . . Keeping legislative business moving is a major service in itself. But leaders are also on the alert for member activities that threaten to earn Congress a bad reputation. (1974, 147)

Mayhew is correct but even the efforts of these "protectors" are unlikely to result in an optimal provision of the collective good. That is, despite the efforts of some legislators to increase public respect for Congress by reforming the institution's worst practices, the effort will be insufficient to restore esteem—the effort will fall far short of producing the types of changes necessary to elevate public confidence in, and respect for, Congress. "This tendency toward sub-optimality is due to the fact that a collective good is, by definition, such that other individuals in the group cannot be kept from consuming it once any individual has provided it for himself. Since an individual member thus gets only part of the benefit of any expenditure he makes to obtain more of the collective good, he will discontinue his purchase of the collective good before the optimal amount for the group as a whole has been obtained" (Olson 1965, 35).

Moreover, the amount of the collective good that a member receives free as a result of the efforts of others further reduces the incentives to provide more of that good at one's own expense. Thus, the cooperation of other members in passing legislative reforms will be difficult to obtain. This forces significant compromises in the legislative process and an inevitable weakening of congressional reforms (e.g., existence of loopholes; see chap. 6). In sum, rarely will legislative reforms survive the congressional process, and when they do they normally will be diluted to assure passage. Hence, such reforms will not supply an optimum amount of change—they will be too watered down to remedy faulty practices or arrangements or to elevate public confidence in the institution and those that serve within.

Monitoring and Punishing Legislators

Another means of controlling rent seeking is by monitoring the behavior of legislators. Monitoring can shed light on the finances of legislators and how they may have profited from assisting special interests in the political process. Of course, there must also be mechanisms that facilitate such monitoring. Congress is relatively rich in this regard, having institutionalized monitoring units within each chamber (i.e., ethics committees) and public disclosure of finances. It seems clear that the existence of these institutionalized mechanisms for monitoring legislator finances and behavior is designed to deter illegal behavior through the fear of being exposed and subsequently punished by one's colleagues.

It is doubtful that these monitoring devices will be very effective in constraining rent seeking. For one thing, congressional committees entrusted with scrutinizing member finances are not highly sought after assignments. Most legislators reluctantly accept membership on the

Ethics Committee as a favor to their party leaders, and they leave at the first chance. This lack of attraction has two important consequences. First, members serving on these committees will have little interest in the subject matter. Hence, shirking by members may arise thereby reducing the time and effort devoted by legislators to their committee responsibilities (i.e., scrutiny of colleagues' behavior).

Second, we can expect that legislators will make few investments in learning the subject matter (ethics laws and rulings) or acquiring expertise. If members do not voluntarily seek membership on the committee and they have no interest in establishing a career on the committee, even if permitted to do so, there are few incentives for members to invest time and energy in acquiring expertise in this area. In fact, we might expect committee members to minimize their investments in a temporary, undesirable assignment, especially given the other committee assignments members also must attend to. The absence of incentives results in little effort in initiating investigations:

> For most of its first two centuries of existence, Congress generally was content to keep its internal affairs undisturbed until outside pressures forced it to act. Occasionally the instigation came from the executive branch, through its Justice Department, which from time to time sued a member of Congress, usually, for income tax evasion. But mainly, as in the 1980s, the pressure for reform was generated by news stories about congressional excesses. (Congressional Quarterly 1992, 145)

In short, congressional monitoring is reactive—it responds only when public exposure, or the efforts of other politicians, forces it to do so. Such conditions are determinantal to effective monitoring.

As for financial disclosure reports, there is no better way to unveil legislator wrongdoings than by allowing public access to a detailed accounting of the sources of legislators' wealth. Public disclosure is intended to provide the information necessary to allow members' constituents to judge their representative's official conduct in light of possible financial conflicts with private holdings. Such public documentation entails a moral hazard: there is no way to assure that individuals engaged in unsavory or unethical practices will reveal this fact through publicly available financial disclosure reports, penalties notwithstanding. In fact, rational legislators engaged in illegal practices will make every effort to conceal their extralegislative pay or benefits. We cannot expect such politicians to ease our task of uncovering malfeasance in office.

Monitoring also must be coupled with sanctions to be effective.

Such sanctions are available in Congress—expulsion and censure. Expulsion is the far more severe punishment: the expelled member is forced from the institution. The Abscam investigation in 1980, in which FBI agents posing as Arab sheiks or businessmen offered bribes to members of Congress, produced the first ouster of a legislator for corruption. Prior to this period, the only grounds on which a member had been expelled was conspiracy against a foreign country and support of a rebellion. For offenses where expulsion is viewed as too severe, Congress punishes its members by reprimanding them in a legislative resolution of censure, requiring only a simple majority vote; expulsion is more exacting and requires a two-thirds majority. In the Senate, censure proceedings are carried out more moderately than they are in the House. The senator accused of wrongdoing, for instance, is allowed to speak in his or her own defense. The House treats their accused with far less civility. Not only are alleged offenders often denied the privilege of addressing the chamber, but censured members are treated like felons: the Speaker of the House calls the person to the front (bar) of the House and issues a solemn pronouncement of censure.

Irrespective of the severity of these punishments, unethical legislators need not be overly concerned since there is a reasonable likelihood of escaping congressional sanctions. In figure 17, I report the rates of success for various sanctions instituted in the House of Representatives. I have included a category for the efforts of Congress to exclude members from taking their seats in the House. This latter category represents attempts by Congress to prevent a member from assuming a position in the institution. The severity of this form of punishment is evident in the fact that the Supreme Court has made significant attempts to constrain this legislative power. Despite the severity of exclusion, legislators have a greater likelihood of being excluded (31.3 percent) than of being expelled (14.3 percent). Expulsion from the House is very unlikely, and even censuring is not a sure thing since almost 40 percent of those subjected to a censure vote escaped punishment. In short, legislators found guilty of violating congressional rules risk punishment, but the risk is not imposing.

The weak incentives for legislators to monitor the finances of their colleagues, the incentives for unethical and corrupt legislators to conceal their gains, and the low probability of institutional punishment diminish the effectiveness of monitoring in constraining rent seeking in Congress. This is not to argue that these mechanisms of monitoring (e.g., financial disclosure reports) are of no avail. I would only contend that such mechanisms have become less effective with the evolution of the rent-seeking society. Their capacity to constrain the types of unethical behavior that

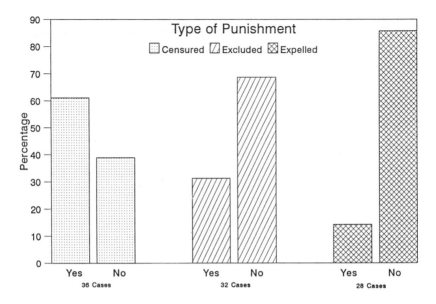

Fig. 17. Rates of punishment in the House of Representatives, 1789–1990. (Data compiled from *Congressional Ethics* 1992, 165–72.)

we have come to expect from rent-seeking legislators remains problematic, at best.

Electoral Control

The ultimate sanction or control is, of course, electoral defeat. The threat of electoral defeat must certainly be realistic to curtail rent-seeking behavior to a significant degree. If electoral defeat is to be a credible deterrent to unethical or illegal behavior, such behavior must be investigated, publicly exposed, and subsequently punished at the polls. The House bank scandal (discussed in chap. 3) exemplifies the first two conditions—the scandal was the object of an internal investigation, and the legislators involved (and their level of involvement) were widely publicized. Some legislators—those with an unusually large number of bank overdrafts—sensed that their involvement in the bank scandal would not sit well with their constituents. Hence, they chose to retire rather than risk the embarrassment (and cost) of a losing campaign: 12 of the 46 House incumbents with 100 or more overdrafts retired in 1992. Few would deny that a legislator's involvement in a scandal costs votes, but the question remains: is the loss sufficient to defeat most entrenched incumbents?

A rather simple measurement of the impact of involvement (or lack thereof) in the House bank scandal on voter support can be obtained by regressing the 1992 vote for House incumbents on three variables: the partisan trend in national forces, the incumbent's level of electoral support in the 1990 (midterm) election, and the number of check overdrafts. The model can be expressed as:

$$V = f(N, E, C), \tag{6}$$

where

$V =$ incumbent's vote percentage in 1992,
$N =$ the effects of partisan national trends—the party identification of the House incumbent (1 if a Democrat and 0 otherwise),
$E =$ incumbent's reelection percentage in 1990—expected level of vote support,
$C =$ number of check overdrafts.

The national-trend variable is designed to capture any pro-Democratic or pro-Republican mood that may have given incumbents an electoral boost or imposed electoral costs in the 1992 election. A good indicator of an incumbent's level of constituency support is the vote percentage received in the most recent midterm election. Midterm elections are less subject to the unpredictable events associated with presidential contests. Hence, they serve as good estimates of an incumbent's expected level of vote support. Finally, if check overdrafters are punished, we can expect a strong negative relationship between the 1992 vote percentage of incumbents and the number of checks bounced.

The estimates of these relationships are shown in table 19. As expected, the electoral votes in 1992 are related to incumbents' votes in 1990, and check overdrafts cost votes. The cost of involvement in a scandal is, however, rather modest: 100 overdrafts would cost an unethical House incumbent about 1 percent of the vote. This is certainly not an outrageous price to pay for unethical behavior, especially given the high levels of electoral safety enjoyed by most House incumbents. Like all of the controls examined in this chapter, the effects of elections are modest at best. If elections were highly competitive, as in earlier historical periods, then the defection of even a small proportion of the electorate might make a big difference in election outcomes. The lack of competition in most congressional elections, however, deprives scandals of a greater electoral impact. Scandals certainly matter in elections but only at the margin, and few congressional districts are electorally marginal (see Fiorina 1977).

In equation 2 (table 19), I substitute a dummy variable that assumes the value of 1 if a legislator kited 100 or more checks at the House bank and zero otherwise, in lieu of the measure of the actual number of kited checks. The inclusion of this dummy variable reflects the possible interactive effect of involvement in a scandal for the most extreme abusers. The interactive effect can be interpreted as capturing the external electoral effects of scandals: those involved attract highly qualified and well-financed opposition at the next election as well as facing an angry electorate. In short, the unusual vulnerability of the biggest abusers at the House bank makes them easy targets.

It should be noted that this formulation results in a rather skewed measurement of the effects of the bank scandal since few legislators kited 100 or more checks. Moreover, this conceptualization attributes *no* electoral effects for the vast majority of the check kiters. The dummy variable's coefficient (table 19, eq. 2) suggests that kiting 100 or more checks costs an incumbent about 6 percent of the vote ($b = -5.8469$).

TABLE 19.   The Electoral Cost of Involvement in the Bank Scandal

Variables	Equation 1			Equation 2		
	b	t-value	Signifi-cance	b	t-value	Signifi-cance
Party identification (N)	.524 (1.433)[a]	.366	.715	.586 (.424)	.411	.681
1990 electoral vote (E)	.237 (.046)	5.140	.000	.243 (.046)	5.277	.000
Number of bank overdrafts (C)	−.012 (.006)	−1.760	.079			
Extreme abuse (100 or more kited checks)				−5.847 (2.497)	−2.341	.020
Statistics						
Multiple R	.30			.32		
R^2	.09			.10		
Standard error	11.55			11.51		
F-statistic	9.41			10.27		
N	282			282		

Source: Data compiled by author.
[a]Standard errors are in parentheses.

While this estimate of the effects of the bank scandal is greater than identified in equation 1 (table 19), the effect remains modest, especially in light of the electoral safety of most incumbents. And despite the higher estimate of the electoral cost of check kiting, this latter model implies that most members were able to escape any punishment for kiting checks at the House bank! In sum, the electoral effects of involvement in the bank scandal are modest at best, and most of those involved were able to withstand voter wrath at the polls. (For additional empirical support of this point, see Groseclose and Krehbiel 1992.)

Summary

The preceding analyses are only suggestive of the problems encountered in attempting to control the behavior of legislators. These controls seem to be designed more to deter legislators from taking advantage of their positions in the legislature than to uncover or punish wrongdoings. Adverse selection hampers the effectiveness of these controls by altering the composition of the legislature so that those occupying the legislature are more difficult to deter from rent seeking. Rent seekers can circumvent the income-reporting procedures involved in financial disclosure laws, and their activities are unlikely to be constrained by the intrinsic returns since the latter have diminished while the size of monetary returns seems to be climbing. Rent seekers also have less to fear from electoral revolt than we might wish: electoral safety has attained very high levels, and voter revolts are rather modest, if not serendipitous, events. While rent seekers risk potential employment opportunities once they leave Congress, the loss in future returns—even very lucrative congressional pensions—cannot rival the sums of money that can be made through rent extractions. Simply put, the size of the monetary returns available and the adverse selection of rent seekers to congressional service make it difficult to constrain rent seeking through the threat of monitoring and punishment, the attractiveness of the intrinsic returns of congressional service, a reduction in postelective office opportunities for employment, or the loss of voter support.

In table 20 I have recorded the mean levels of campaign expenditures and receipts between 1983 and 1990 by those who have accepted honoraria in 1989–90 ("rent seekers") and those House incumbents who reported no honoraria earnings ("non–rent seekers") during this period. These data suggest that rent seekers are spending more heavily to hold on to their seats in the House and obtaining more funds for that purpose than are non–rent seekers. Non–rent seekers, in contrast, reveal no major increases in either campaign expenditures or receipts. Moreover, the

TABLE 20.   Campaign Expenditures and Receipts and the Demand for Rents, 1983–90, in 1982 Dollars

	Campaign Expenditures		Campaign Receipts	
	Rent Seekers	Non–Rent Seekers	Rent Seekers	Non–Rent Seekers
1983–84	255,203	224,592	295,990	261,675
1985–86	278,757	226,970	320,636*	256,905
1987–88	285,297*	222,893	336,681*	257,460
1989–90	297,674*	225,240	333,571*	251,495

Source: Federal Election Commission Reports 1983–90.

*Statistically significant difference between rent seekers and non–rent seekers at .05 level (two-tailed test).

differences seem to be growing. These data also suggest that rent-seeking behavior (e.g., raising large campaign war chests and overspending to gain reelection) is not being effectively constrained by existing controls on legislators. Present controls on the rent-seeking behavior of legislators may be ineffective because rent seekers stand to gain so much from their actions. Hence, they—rent seekers—heavily discount the deterrent effects that reflect the force of present controls on legislators.

Structural reform of institutional arrangements might stifle rent seeking in Congress to some degree, but if adverse selection affects institutional evolution these efforts will encounter a great deal of difficulty in achieving any lofty goals. It is tempting to offer some prescriptions that might be successful in constraining rent seeking, but I cannot envision any set of institutional arrangements that could guarantee such an effect. The simple answer in this regard is to increase the intrinsic returns to congressional service while assuring declines in the material returns and gains from rent-seeking behavior. How institutional arrangements might be modified or created to accomplish these twin objectives is beyond the scope of this inquiry. I only hope that this analysis will better inform those involved and influential in designing institutional remedies of the magnitude of the problem.

Conclusion

I conclude this study with a brief summary of the major ideas and findings presented in it. Aside from the assumption common to most public choice approaches—namely, that legislators are rational utility-maximizers—this study is guided by three additional assumptions designed to reflect the impact of a rent-seeking society (and rent seeking, in particular) on political institutions: long service in politics reflects one's preference for the intrinsic, rather than the material, rewards of public service; the intrinsic returns to officeholding accrue value with tenure in the job, all things being equal; and rent-seeking behavior in a legislature reduces the intrinsic returns to a congressional career. These model assumptions yield four hypotheses describing the entry and exit of career politicians and the changes over time in rent-seeking behavior in Congress:

1. Rent seekers are more inclined than others to manipulate institutional arrangements for financial gain, thereby precipitating scandals
2. Rent seeking reduces the intrinsic returns from officeholding to the point that those who value these returns the most enter Congress in decreasing proportions. This alters the composition of the institution so that those who value other rewards—namely, financial gain—become more dominant within an institution
3. Newer generations of legislators engage in rent-seeking behavior to a greater degree than older cohorts
4. Declines in the intrinsic returns of a congressional career result in the departure of career legislators

All of the above hypotheses received empirical support. Specifically, rent-seeking activity among congressional incumbents has increased over time in terms of campaign spending and fund-raising, with incumbents elected prior to the 1970s exhibiting the lowest levels of rent seeking. High levels of rent seeking and low levels of institutional esteem apparently deter career politicians from seeking congressional office. In addition, weak controls and punishments mark legislative life. Controls on the unethical behavior of legislators are designed only to deter such behavior. They are exceedingly weak in either uncovering or punishing unethical legislators. Indeed, the empirical evidence suggests a significant, but not a substantial, effect of these controls: (1) check kiting had only a marginal impact on the electoral vote in 1992, probably because high barriers to entry create large incumbent election victories, (2) punishment rates in the House seem insufficient in deterring unethical behavior, and (3) postelective job opportunities are reduced for those legislators involved in scandals although the loss is rather slight— only about one less job opportunity over a ten-year period.

I also presented evidence suggesting that rent seeking is not constrained by seniority. Theoretically, increased tenure should lead to higher levels of consumption of intrinsic returns and less rent-seeking behavior. However, I found rent-seeking behavior increasing across all congressional cohorts, especially recent cohorts. Even at the same point in their congressional careers and correcting for changes in the value of the U.S. dollar, newer generations raise and spend more campaign funds than the most senior congressional cohort—a symptom of adverse selection.

In figure 18 I describe the hypothetical intrinsic and material returns that legislators can expect during the course of their congressional careers. The returns from rent seeking, as noted earlier, conform to the principle of diminishing marginal productivity. Hence, the rents received from such behavior should follow a similar path. That is, rents (R) are expected to increase until some point (A) after which they begin to slowly decline both in total and marginal returns. At some point (B) after rents begin to decline, the intrinsic returns from a congressional career rise beyond the material returns from rent seeking, thereby encouraging legislators to consume more of the intrinsic returns and to curb (or even diminish) rent-seeking behavior (I).

These two curves (R and I) start at about the same point, that is, at the entry of a legislator. New legislators must work extremely hard during their early years in office to strengthen their electoral safety within their districts. Their relatively low status in Congress restricts the rents they collect because most business goes to low-cost suppliers who usually can boast of longer tenure (chap. 5). Moreover, their concern over reelection constrains their consumption of the intrinsic returns. As tenure increases, so do the rents available for capture; and the intrinsic returns also rise, but more gradually. Therefore, no matter how attractive the consumption of the intrinsic returns might be, the

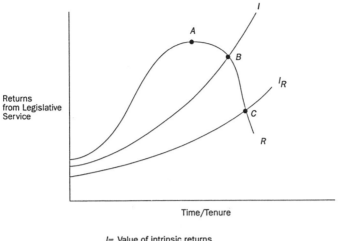

I= Value of intrinsic returns
I$_R$= Impact of rent seeking on the intrinsic returns
R= Returns from rent seeking

Fig. 18. Intrinsic and rent-seeking returns from legislative service

lure of rent seeking is probably even more attractive, especially for new members. Hence, these legislators devote their efforts to the enterprise with the greatest return—namely, rent seeking. At some point, the consumption of the intrinsic returns exceeds the returns from rent seeking, and legislators increase their consumption at the expense of rent seeking.

One of the effects of the rent-seeking society is to diminish these intrinsic returns thereby producing a flatter curve (I_R) that exceeds the returns from rent seeking (R) at a point farther down the curve tracing rent-seeking returns (C). Under this latter condition, rent seeking can be expected to continue for a longer period of time before the value of the intrinsic returns exceeds the returns from rent-seeking behavior. Thus, the more we degrade the Congress, the more we increase the probability that the legislature will evolve in ways destined to further reduce the intrinsic returns of congressional service, thereby encouraging rather than constraining rent seeking.[1] Fortunately, the legislature has not

---

1. There seems to be something of a vicious circle here: scandals lower institutional esteem so that Congress is unable to attract highly reputable career politicians, and low levels of institutional esteem result from attracting rent seekers to legislative service. What

degenerated to the point that rent-seeking behavior accelerates with retirement decisions. I found no evidence of opportunistic, rent-seeking behavior in the "last period" of officeholding. Last-period problems might be less important at this point in time because career legislators seem to be exiting Congress. Since these careerists have invested heavily in their reputations over the years and desire to pursue employment opportunities upon leaving office they are unlikely to engage in behavior that might tarnish their images.

Taken together, these findings are consistent with the premise that adverse selection can emerge to affect the evolution of political institutions in a rent-seeking society. It may be extremely difficult to free our institutions from the externalities created by a rent-seeking society, but it will be far more difficult to do so if we do not recognize the nature of the problem and the damaging effects it could have on the U.S. Congress. I hope that this inquiry enhances such an awareness.

It may be that good men and women enter Congress only to be corrupted by the enormous amounts of money involved in obtaining political influence. I would not deny this possibility, though it seems impossible to test empirically. I would add, however, that as painful as it might be we need to entertain the possibility that adverse selection may also be at work. If so, institutional remedies will need to involve more than just tinkering with legislative arrangements; attention needs to be given to the long-term effects of a rent-seeking society on the evolution of political institutions.

I do not want to fall victim to the same unjustifiable concern that led Henny Penny to sound the alarm that the "sky is falling." I prefer to think of the message of this study as urging attention to a potential problem in the evolution of the U.S. Congress. I have assembled evidence to suggest that the symptoms of adverse selection appear to be surfacing. I would not claim, however, that adverse selection is presently a serious problem in the evolution of Congress since none of the findings are without important caveats. But even if adverse selection has not reached a critical threshold, we need to vigilantly monitor and analyze its symptoms. To do otherwise is to ignore the obvious—rent-seeking activities corrupt institutional arrangements and destroy public respect for political structures and elites. The alarm I sound seems equivalent to

---

is likely to transpire under these conditions is that the market for "good" politicians will come to resemble Akerlof's characterization of the market for "good" used cars: "there tends to be a reduction in the average quality of goods and also in the size of the market" (1970, 488). How such a circle might be broken is beyond the scope of this inquiry, but it is clear that the level of institutional esteem is a critical factor. Hence, restoring institutional esteem seems a pivotal objective in any effort to break the circle.

the risk we assume in ignoring the emerging symptoms of adverse selection. These symptoms may not portend the decline of Congress as an effective representational institution, but before these patterns are passed off as mere intellectual fancy, it may be useful to ponder the message inscribed on a granite tombstone in a small cemetery in Key West, Florida: "I told you I was really sick"!

References

Aberbach, Joel D., and Bert A. Rockman. 1978. "Bureaucrats and Clientele Groups: A View from Capitol Hill." *American Journal of Political Science* 22: 818–32.

Akerlof, George A. 1970. "The Market for 'Lemons': Quality Uncertainty and the Market Mechanism." *Quarterly Journal of Economics* 84: 488–500.

Alchian, Armen A. 1950. "Uncertainty, Evolution and Economic Theory." *Journal of Political Economy* 58: 211–21.

Alchian, Armen A., and Harold Demsetz. 1972. "Production, Information Costs, and Economic Organization." *American Economic Review* 62: 777–95.

American Enterprise. 1992. 3, no. 6 (November/December).

Asher, Herbert B. 1973. "The Learning of Legislative Norms." *American Political Science Review* 67: 499–513.

Barber, James D. 1965. *The Lawmakers*. New Haven, Conn.: Yale University Press.

Barro, Robert J. 1973. "The Control of Politicians: An Economic Model." *Public Choice* 14: 19–42.

Becker, Gary S. 1983. "A Theory of Competition Among Pressure Groups for Political Influence." *Quarterly Journal of Economics* 98: 371–400.

Becker, Gary S. 1985. "Public Policies, Pressure Groups, and Dead Weight Costs." *Journal of Public Economics* 28: 329–47.

Becker, Gary S., and George Stigler. 1988. "Law Enforcement, Malfeasance, and the Compensation of Enforcers." In *Chicago Studies in Political Economy*, ed. George Stigler, 593–611. Chicago: University of Chicago Press.

Bentley, Arthur. 1908. *The Process of Government*. Chicago: University of Chicago Press.

Bennett, James T., and Thomas J. DiLorenzo. 1982. "The Political Economy of Political Philosophy: Discretionary Spending by Senators on Staff." *American Economic Review* 72: 1153–61.

Ben-zion, Uri, and Zeev Eytan. 1974. "On Money, Votes, and Policy in a Democratic Society." *Public Choice* 17: 1–10.

Berry, Jeffrey M. 1984. *The Interest Group Society*. Boston: Little, Brown.

Born, Richard. 1979. "Generational Replacement and the Growth of Incumbent Reelection Margins in the U.S. House." *American Political Science Review* 73: 811–17.

Brace, Paul. 1984. "Progressive Ambition in the House: A Probabilistic Approach." *Journal of Politics* 46: 556–71.

Buchanan, James. 1980. "Rent Seeking and Profit Seeking." In *Toward a Theory of the Rent-Seeking Society*, ed. James M. Buchanan, Robert D. Tollison, and Gordon Tullock, 3–15. College Station, Tex.: Texas A&M University Press.

Buchanan, James M., Robert D. Tollison, and Gordon Tullock, eds. 1980. *Toward a Theory of the Rent-Seeking Society.* College Station, Tex.: Texas A&M University Press.

Buchanan, James M., and Gordon Tullock. 1962. *The Calculus of Consent.* Ann Arbor: University of Michigan Press.

Burnham, Walter D. 1975. "Insulation and Responsiveness in Congressional Elections." *Political Science Quarterly* 90: 411–35.

Canon, David T. 1990. *Actors, Athletes, and Astronauts.* Chicago: University of Chicago Press.

Chappell, Henry W., Jr. 1982. "Campaign Contributions and Congressional Voting." *Review of Economics and Statistics* 64: 77–83.

Coase, Ronald H. 1960. "The Problem of Social Cost." *Journal of Law and Economics* 3: 1–44.

Committee on Standards of Official Conduct, U.S. House of Representatives. 1992. "Historical Summary of Conduct Cases in the House of Representatives." Committee print, April.

Congressional Ethics. 1992. Washington, D.C.: Congressional Quarterly.

Congressional Quarterly. 1992. *Congressional Quarterly Weekly Report,* April 18, 106–7.

Congressional Quarterly. 1992. *Congressional Quarterly Weekly Report,* April 4, 859.

Cooper, Joseph, and William West. 1981. "Voluntary Retirement, Incumbency, and the Modern House." *Political Science Quarterly* 96: 279–300.

Cox, Gary W., and Matthew D. McCubbins. 1993. *Legislative Leviathan.* Berkeley: University of California.

Craig, Stephen C. 1993. *The Malevolent Leaders.* Boulder, Colo.: Westview Press.

Crain, Mark, Donald Leavens, and Robert Tollison. 1986. "Final Voting in Legislatures." *American Economic Review* 76: 833–41.

Davidson, Roger H., and Walter J. Oleszek. 1977. *Congress Against Itself.* Bloomington, Ind.: Indiana University Press.

Denzau, Arthur T., and Michael C. Munger. 1986. "Legislators and Interest Groups: How Unorganized Interests Get Represented." *American Political Science Review* 80: 89–106.

Dougan, William R., and Michael C. Munger. 1989. "The Rationality of Ideology." *Journal of Law and Economics* 32: 119–42.

Downs, Anthony. 1957. *An Economic Theory of Democracy.* New York: Harper and Row.

Eckert, Ross. 1981. "The Life Cycle of Regulatory Commissioners." *Journal of Law and Economics* 24: 113–20.

Endersby, James, and Michael Munger. 1992. "The Impact of Legislator Attributes on Union PAC Campaign Contributions." *Journal of Labor Research* 13: 79–97.

Evans, Diana M. 1986. "PAC Contributions and Roll–Call Voting: Conditional Power." In *Interest Group Politics,* 2d ed., Allan J. Cigler and Burdett A. Loomis, 114–29. Washington, D.C.: Congressional Quarterly.

Faith, Roger, Donald Leavens, and Robert Tollison. 1982. "Anti–Trust Pork Barrel." *Journal of Law and Economics* 25: 329–342.

Federal Election Commission Report. 1981–90. Washington, D.C.

Federalist Papers, The, No. 10. 1961. New York: New American Library.

Fenno, Richard F., Jr. 1973. *Congressmen in Committees.* Boston: Little, Brown.

Fenno, Richard F., Jr. 1978. *Home Style.* Boston: Little, Brown.

Ferejohn, John. 1986. "Incumbent Performance and Electoral Control." *Public Choice* 50: 5–25.

Fiorina, Morris. 1978. "Economic Retrospective Voting in American National Elections: A Micro Analysis." *American Journal of Political Science* 22: 426–43.

Fiorina, Morris P. 1977. *Congress: Keystone of the Washington Establishment.* New Haven, Conn.: Yale University Press.

Fowler, Linda L., and Robert D. McClure. 1989. *Political Ambition: Who Decides to Run for Congress.* New Haven, Conn.: Yale University Press.

Frantzich, Stephen E. 1978. "DeRecruitment: The Other Side of the Congressional Equation." *Western Political Quarterly* 31: 105–26.

Froehlich, Norman, Joe A. Oppenheimer, and Oran R. Young. 1971. *Political Leadership and Collective Goods.* Princeton, N.J.: Princeton University Press.

Garmant, Suzanne. 1991. *Scandals: The Crisis of Mistrust in American Politics.* New York: Times Books.

General Social Surveys. 1973–91. National Opinion Research Center, University of Chicago.

Gertzog, Irwin N. 1976. "The Routinization of Committee Assignments in the U.S. House of Representatives." *American Journal of Political Science* 20: 693–712.

Gilligan, Thomas W., William J. Marshall, and Barry R. Weingast. 1989. "Regulation and the Theory of Legislative Choice: The Interstate Commerce Act of 1887." *Journal of Law and Economics* 32: 35–61.

Glazer, Amihai. 1993. "On the Incentives to Establish and Play Political Rent–Seeking." *Public Choice* 75: 139–48.

Goldenberg, Eddie N., and Michael W. Traugott. 1984. *Campaigning for Congress.* Washington, D.C.: Congressional Quarterly Press.

Goldstone, Jack A. 1975. "Subcommittee Chairmanships in the House of Representatives." *American Political Science Review* 69: 970–71.

Gopoian, J. David. 1948. "What Makes PACs Tick? An Analysis of the Allocation Patterns of Economic Interest Groups." *American Journal of Political Science* 28: 259–81.

Grier, Kevin, Michael Munger, and Brian Roberts. 1991. "The Industrial Organization of Corporate Political Participation." *Southern Economic Journal* 57: 727–38.

Grier, Kevin, and Michael Munger. 1993. "Comparing Interest Group PAC Contributions to House and Senate Incumbents, 1980–1986." *Journal of Politics* 55: 615–43.

Groseclose, Timothy, and Keith Krehbiel. 1992. "Golden Parachutes, Rubber Checks, and Strategic Retirements from the 102nd House." Unpublished manuscript, Stanford University.

Grenzke, Janet M. 1989. "PACs and the Congressional Supermarket: The Currency Is Complex." *American Journal of Political Science* 33: 1–24.

Herndon, James F. 1982. "Access, Record, and Competition As Influences on Interest Group Contributions to Congressional Campaigns." *Journal of Politics* 44: 996–1019.

Hibbing, John. 1982a. "Voluntary Retirement from the House: The Costs of Congressional Service." *Legislative Studies Quarterly* 7: 57–74.

Hibbing, John. 1982b. "Voluntary Retirement from the U.S. House of Representatives: Who Quits?" *American Journal of Political Science* 26: 467–484.

Huitt, Ralph K. 1961. "The Outsider In The Senate." *American Political Science Review* 55: 566–575.

Jacobson, Gary C. 1990. *The Electoral Origins of Divided Government.* Boulder, Colo.: Westview Press.

Jensen, Michael C., and William H. Meckling. 1976. "Theory of the Firm: Managerial Behavior, Agency Costs, and Ownership Structure." *Journal of Financial Economics* 3: 305–60.

Kalt, Joseph P., and Mark A. Zupan. 1984. "Capture and Ideology in the Economic Theory of Politics." *American Economic Review* 74: 279–300.

Kalt, Joseph P., and Mark A. Zupan. 1990. "The Apparent Ideological Behavior of Legislatures: Testing for Principal–Agent Slack in Political Institutions." *Journal of Law and Economics* 33: 103–31.

Kaplan, Abraham. 1964. *The Conduct of Inquiry.* San Francisco: Chandler Publishing.

Kau, James B., and Paul H. Rubin. 1979. "Self–Interest, Ideology, and Logrolling in Congressional Voting." *Journal of Law and Economics* 22: 365–84.

Kau, James B., and Paul H. Rubin. 1982. *Congressmen, Constituents, and Contributors.* Boston: Martinus Nijhoff.

Keim, Gerald, and Asghar Zardkoohi. 1988. "Looking for Leverage in PAC Markets: Corporate and Labor Contributions Considered." *Public Choice* 58: 21–34.

Klein, Benjamin, Robert G. Crawford, and Armen A. Alchian. 1978. "Vertical Integration, Appropriate Rents, and the Competitive Contracting Process." *Journal of Law and Economics* 21: 297–326.

Klein, Benjamin, and Keith B. Leffler. 1981. "The Role of Market Forces in Assuring Contractual Performance." *Journal of Political Economy* 89: 615–41.

Krueger, Anne O. 1974. "The Political Economy of the Rent–Seeking Society." *American Economic Review* 64: 291–303.

Landes, William, and Richard A. Posner. 1975. "The Independent Judiciary in an Interest–Group Perspective." *Journal of Law and Economics* 18: 875–901.

Langbein, Laura I. 1986. "Money and Access: Some Empirical Evidence." *Journal of Politics* 48: 1052–62.

Lipset, Seymour, and William Schneider. 1983. *Confidence Gap.* New York: Free Press.

Livingston, Steven, and Sally Friedman. 1993. "Reexamining Theories of Congressional Retirement: Evidence from the 1980s." *Legislative Studies Quarterly* 18: 231–253.

Lott, John R. 1987. "Political Cheating." *Public Choice* 52: 169–87.

Lott, John R. 1990. "Attendance Rates, Political Shirking, and the Effect of Post–Elective Office Employment." *Economic Inquiry* 28: 133–50.

Lott, John R., and Michael Davis. 1992. "A Critical Review and An Extension of the Political Shirking Literature." *Public Choice* 74: 461–84.

Lott, John R., and Robert W. Reed. 1989. "Shirking and Sorting in a Political Market with Finite–lived Politicians." *Public Choice* 61: 75–96.

Lowi, Theodore J. 1969. *The End of Liberalism.* New York: W. W. Norton.

Matlack, Carol, and Jennifer Casper. 1989. "Surveying Trade Group Salaries." *National Journal,* February 18, 410–13.

Matthews, Donald R. 1973. *U.S. Senators and Their World.* New York: W. W. Norton.

Mayhew, David R. 1974. *Congress: The Electoral Connection.* New Haven, Conn.: Yale University Press.

McChesney, Fred S. 1987. "Rent Extraction and Rent Creation in the Economic Theory of Regulation." *Journal of Legal Studies* 16: 101–18.

McCormick, Robert E., and Robert D. Tollison. 1980. "Wealth Transfers in a Representative Democracy." In *Toward a Theory of the Rent–Seeking Society,* ed. James M. Buchanan, Robert D. Tollison, and Gordon Tullock, 293–313. College Station, Tex.: Texas A&M University Press.

McCormick, Robert E., and Robert D. Tollison. 1981. *Politicians, Legislation, and the Economy.* Boston: Martinus Nijhoff.

Merck, Carolyn. 1993. "Benefit and Pay Increases in Selected Federal Programs, 1969–1994." Congressional Research Service, Library of Congress, November 19.

Merida, Kevin. 1994. "It'll Take an Act of Congress to Clean Up Its Image." *Washington Post, National Weekly Edition,* February 7–13, 13–14.

Milbrath, Lester W. 1963. *The Washington Lobbyists.* Chicago: Rand McNally.

Miller, Gary, and Terry Moe. 1983. "Bureaucrats, Legislators, and the Size of Government." *American Political Science Review* 77: 297–322.

Mitchell, William C., and Michael C. Munger. 1991. "Economic Models of Interest Groups: An Introductory Survey." *American Journal of Political Science* 35: 512–46.

Moe, Terry M. 1980. *The Organization of Interests*. Chicago: University of Chicago Press.

Moe, Terry M. 1984. "The New Economics of Organization." *American Journal of Political Science* 28: 739–77.

Moore, Michael K., and John Hibbing. 1992. "Is Serving in Congress Fun Again? Voluntary Retirements from the House Since the 1970s." *American Journal of Political Science* 36: 824–28.

Mueller, Dennis C. 1989. *Public Choice II*. New York: Cambridge University Press.

National Election Studies. 1969–86. University of Michigan, Ann Arbor, Michigan.

Nelson, Douglas, and Eugene Silberberg. 1987. "Ideology and Legislator Shirking." *Economic Inquiry* 25: 15–25.

Nelson, Phillip. 1974. "Advertising as Information." *Journal of Political Economy* 82: 729–54.

Olson, Mancur. 1965. *The Logic of Collective Action*. Cambridge, Mass.: Harvard University Press.

Ornstein, Norman J., and Shirley Elder. 1978. *Interest Groups, Lobbying and Policy–Making*. Washington, D.C.: Congressional Quarterly.

Ornstein, Norman, Thomas Mann, and Michael Malbin. 1990. *Vital Statistics on Congress, 1989–1990*. Washington, D.C.: Congressional Quarterly.

Orr, Daniel. 1980. "Rent Seeking in an Aging Population." In *Toward a Theory of the Rent-Seeking Society*, ed. James M. Buchanan, Robert D. Tollison, and Gordon Tullock, 222–34. College Station, Tex.: Texas A&M University Press.

Palmore, Erdman. 1978. "When Can Age, Period, and Cohort be Separated?" *Social Forces*, 282–95.

Parker, Glenn R. 1986. *Homeward Bound*. Pittsburgh: University of Pittsburgh Press.

Parker, Glenn. 1989a. "The Role of Constituency Trust in Congressional Elections." *Public Opinion Quarterly* 53: 175–96.

Parker, Glenn R. 1989b. *Characteristics of Congress*. Englewood Cliffs, N.J.: Prentice-Hall.

Parker, Glenn R. 1992a. *Institutional Change, Discretion, and the Making of Modern Congress: An Economic Interpretation*. Ann Arbor: University of Michigan Press.

Parker, Glenn R. 1992b. "The Distribution of Honoraria Income in the U.S. Congress: Who Gets Rents in Legislatures and Why?" *Public Choice* 73: 167–81.

Parker, Glenn R., and Suzanne Parker. 1985. *Factions in House Committees*. Knoxville: University of Tennessee Press.

Parker, Suzanne, and Glenn R. Parker. 1993. "Why Do We Trust Our Congressman?" *Journal of Politics* 55: 442–53.

Peltzman, Sam. 1976. "Toward A More General Theory of Regulation." *Journal of Law and Economics* 19: 211–40.

Peltzman, Sam. 1984. "Constituent Interest and Congressional Voting." *Journal of Law and Economics* 27: 181–210.

Pittman, Russell. 1977. "Market Structure and Campaign Contributions." *Public Choice* 31: 37–52.

Polsby, Nelson W. 1968. "The Institutionalization of the U.S. House of Representatives." *American Political Science Review* 62: 144–68.

Posner, Richard A. 1980. "The Social Costs of Monopoly and Regulation." In *Toward a Theory of the Rent-Seeking Society,* ed. James M. Buchanan, Robert D. Tollison, and Gordon Tullock, 71–94. College Station, Tex.: Texas A&M University Press.

Posner, Richard A. 1974. "Theories of Economic Regulation." *Bell Journal of Economics and Management Science* 5: 335–58.

Prewitt, Kenneth. 1970. *The Recruitment of Political Leaders: A Study of Citizen-Politicians.* Indianapolis: Bobbs-Merrill.

Report of the 1989 Commission on Executive, Legislative and Judicial Salaries. 1988. *Fairness For Our Public Servants.* Washington, D.C.: Government Printing Office, December 15.

Rohde, David, Norman J. Ornstein, and Robert L. Peabody. 1985. "Political Change and Legislative Norms in the U.S. Senate, 1957–1974." In *Studies of Congress,* ed. Glenn R. Parker, 147–88. Washington, D.C.: Congressional Quarterly.

Roper Surveys, Study #76–8, August 1976.

Rose-Ackerman, Susan. 1978. *Corruption.* New York: Academic Press.

Roster of United States Congressional Officeholder and Biographical Characteristics of Members of the United States Congress, 1789–1991 (ICPSR, Study #7803). 1991. Inter-University Consortium for Political and Social Research, University of Michigan.

Sabato, Larry J. 1984. *PAC Power: Inside the World of Political Action Committees.* New York: W. W. Norton.

Salisbury, Robert H. 1969. "An Exchange Theory of Interest Groups." *Midwest Journal of Political Science* 13: 1–32.

Schattschneider, E. E. 1975. *The Semisovereign People.* Hinsdale, Ill.: Dryden Press.

Schlesinger, Joseph A. 1966. *Ambition and Politics: Political Careers in the United States.* Chicago: Rand McNally.

Sherrill, Robert. 1974. *Why They Call It Politics.* New York: Harcourt Brace Jovanovich.

Shughart, William F., II, and Robert D. Tollison. 1981. "Corporate Chartering: An Exploration in the Economics of Legal Change." *Economic Inquiry* 23: 585–99.

Silberman, Jonathan, and Gilbert Yochum. 1980. "The Market for Special Interest Campaign Funds: An Exploratory Approach." *Public Choice* 35: 75–83.

Smith, Richard A. 1984. "Advocacy, Interpretation, and Influence in the U.S. Congress." *American Political Science Review* 78: 44–63.

Stigler, George. 1971. "The Theory of Economic Regulation." *Bell Journal of Economics and Management Science* 2: 3–21.

Stigler, George. 1972. "Economic and Political Competition." *Public Choice* 13: 91–106.

Stigler, George. Preface to *Chicago Studies in Political Economy,* ed. George Stigler, ix–xviii. Chicago: University of Chicago Press.

Thompson, Dennis F. 1993. "Mediated Corruption: The Case of the Keating Five." *American Political Science Review* 87: 369–81.

Tiebout, Charles M. 1956. "A Pure Theory of Local Expenditures." *Journal of Political Economy* 64: 416–24.

Tollison, Robert D. 1982. "Rent Seeking: A Survey." *Kyklos* 35: 575–602.

Tollison, Robert D. 1993. "Rent Seeking." Unpublished manuscript.

Truman, David B. 1951. *The Governmental Process.* New York: Alfred A. Knopf.

Tullock, Gordon. 1980a. "The Transitional Gains Trap." In *Toward a Theory of the Rent-Seeking Society,* ed. James M. Buchanan, Robert D. Tollison, and Gordon Tullock, 211–21. College Station, Tex.: Texas A&M University Press.

Tullock, Gordon. 1980b. "The Welfare Costs of Tariffs, Monopolies, and Theft." In *Toward a Theory of the Rent-Seeking Society,* ed. James M. Buchanan, Robert D. Tollison, and Gordon Tullock, 39–50. College Station, Tex.: Texas A&M University Press.

U.S. House Commission on Administrative Review. 1977a. *Hearings on Financial Ethics.* 95th Cong., 1st sess., January 13, 14, 31 and February 2, 297.

U.S. House Commission on Administrative Review. 1977b. *Final Report of the Commission on Administrative Review.* 95th Cong., 2d sess., H. Doc. 95–276.

Vedder, Richard, and Lowell Gallaway. 1991. "The War Between the Rent Seekers." *Public Choice* 68: 283–89.

Walker, Jack L. 1983. "The Origins and Maintenance of Interest Groups in America." *American Political Science Review* 77: 390–406.

Washington Post, National Weekly Edition. 1992. September 14–20, 34.

Weingast, Barry, and William Marshall. 1988. "The Industrial Organization of Congress; or, Why Legislatures, Like Firms, Are Not Organized as Markets." *Journal of Political Economy* 96: 132–63.

Welch, William P. 1980. "The Allocation of Political Monies: Economic Interest Groups." *Public Choice* 35: 97–120.

Wilson, James Q. 1973. *Political Organizations.* New York: Basic Books.

Wolanin, Thomas R. 1974. "Committee Seniority and the Choice of House Subcommittee Chairman: 80th–91st Congresses." *Journal of Politics* 36: 687–702.

Wright, John R. 1990. "Contributions, Lobbying, and Committee Voting in the U.S. House of Representatives." *American Political Science Review* 84: 417–38.

Wright, John R. 1985. "PACs, Contributions and Roll Calls: An Organizational Perspective." *American Political Science Review* 79: 400–14.

Wyrick, Thomas L., and Robert A. Arnold. 1989. "Earmarking As A Deterrent to Rent-Seeking." *Public Choice* 60: 283–91.

Zupan, Mark A. 1990. "The Last-Period Problem in Politics: Do Congressional Representatives Not Subject to a Reelection Constraint Alter Their Voting Behavior? *Public Choice* 65: 167–80.

Name Index

Aberbach, Joel D., 65
Akerlof, George A., 48, 66, 156
Alchian, Armen A., 15, 58, 64, 66–67, 132, 139
Asher, Herbert B., 59

Barber, James D., 5, 45, 59
Barro, Robert J., 136, 140
Becker, Gary S., 11, 26, 31, 135
Bennett, James T., 62
Benson, Bruce, vii
Bentley, Arthur, 11
Biaggi, Mario, (D-N.Y.), 126
Buchanan, James M., 1, 6, 14, 15, 65

Canon, David T., 6, 38, 45, 83, 84, 90
Casper, Jennifer, 39
Chappell, Henry W., Jr., 33
Cooper, Joseph, 117, 118, 119, 120, 121
Cox, Gary W., 76
Craig, Stephen C., 38, 69
Crawford, Robert G., 15, 132

Davidson, Roger H., 8, 76, 84n
Davis, Michael, 57, 124
Day, Colin, vii
Demsetz, Harold, 58, 139
Denzau, Arthur T., 11, 27, 28, 46, 59
DiLorenzo, Thomas J., 62
Dougan, William R., 136
Downs, Anthony, 15–16n, 21–22, 29, 30, 131, 136
Duncan, John, (R-Tenn.), 126

Eckert, Ross, 21
Endersby, James, 28
Evans, Diana M., 33

Faith, Roger, 58
Fenno, Richard F., Jr., vii, 5, 59, 63, 123, 143, 150
Fiorina, Morris, vii, 18, 58, 64, 67
Fowler, Linda L., 90
Frantzich, Stephen E., 117, 131
Friedman, Sally, 119
Fuqua, Don, (D-Fla.), 125n

Gallaway, Lowell, 27
Garcia, Robert, (D-N.Y.), 126
Gertzog, Irwin N., 76
Gilligan, Thomas W., 24, 65
Glazer, Amihai, 41
Goldenberg, Eddie N., 65
Goldstone, Jack A., 143
Gopoian, J. David, 95
Grenzke, Janet M., 34
Grier, Kevin, 26, 100
Groseclose, Timothy, 151

Hastings, Warren, British Governor General of India, 74
Hibbing, John, 40, 69, 117, 119, 120, 121
Howard, James, (D-N.J.), 126
Huitt, Ralph K., 77

Jacobson, Gary C., 38, 90

Kalt, Joseph P., 63, 131, 135
Kaplan, Abraham, 37
Keating, Charles, 51
Keim, Gerald, 34
Klein, Benjamin, 15, 98, 101, 132, 139

Subject Index

Adverse selection, 3, 53, 65–67, 90, 107, 123, 152
  generational changes in campaign spending, 102–4
  House bank scandal, 57–58, 62, 64
  hypotheses, 43–44, 48–49, 153
  institutional effects of, 67–68, 151
  model for studying, 37, 153
  in recruitment to Congress, 81–90
  role of public esteem, 68–74, 103
  structure of Congress, 57–58, 74–81

Campaign spending
  analysis of campaign expenditures, 109–12
  analysis of campaign receipts, 112–13
  changes in, 107–13
  in last period, 127–32
  See also Rent seeking
Cohort analysis, 105–9
  campaign expenditures, 109–12
  campaign receipts, 112–13
  See also Campaign spending
Congressional salaries, 140–41
Congressional scandals, 51–53
  See also House bank scandal

Diminishing marginal product, 46–47, 102–3, 154

Externalities, 3

Federal Election Campaign Act, 124–26

Free-rider problem
  collective goods (in Congress), 144–45
  congressional reforms, 144

Group size in politics, 29–33

Honoraria
  analysis of honoraria earnings, 99–102
  House of Representatives, 99–101
  impact of structure of Congress, 96–102
  low-cost suppliers, 96–98, 100, 101
  price premiums, 98, 101
  restrictions on, 95–96
  Senate, 99–101
  shirking, 99
House bank scandal
  check kiting described, 54–56
  effects on reelection, 148–51
  explanations for, 56–60
  implications, 64
  public perceptions of, 52
  statistical analysis, 60–63

Institutional esteem, 6, 41, 43, 143–44
  See also Adverse selection; Intrinsic returns
Institutional evolution, 1, 66, 67–68, 152, 156
Intrinsic returns, 3–4, 6, 7, 37–43, 63–64, 103
  amateur politicians, 44–45, 82–88